April 5, 1984

For dea~ ... ... ery special

... ... Wishes

LORETTE WILMOT LIBRARY
Nazareth College of Rochester

Earl Kage

BALI
BEHIND THE MASK

BALI
BEHIND THE MASK

ANA DANIEL

WITH A FOREWORD BY R. BUCKMINSTER FULLER

ALFRED A. KNOPF/NEW YORK/1981

Library of Congress Cataloging in Publication Data

Daniel, Ana.

Bali, behind the mask.

Bibliography: p.

1. Dancing—Indonesia—Bali (Island).   2.   Bali
(Island)—Social life and customs.   I.   Title.

GV1703.I532B343 1980   793.3'19598'6   79-3481

ISBN 0-394-50264-7

ISBN 0-394-73844-6 (pbk.)

Manufactured in the United States of America

First Edition

All photographs were taken by the author except for the following:

page xviii: Henri Cartier-Bresson, 1954

xxi: Phillipe Genty, 1973

2: Mark Poffenberger, 1978

Frontispiece: Chamber interior, Gunung Kawi

This book was set in a film version of Palatino, originally designed by Hermann Zapf.
Composed by Monotype Composition Company, Baltimore, Maryland. Printed by Rae Publishing, Inc.,
Cedar Grove, New Jersey. Color separations by Offset Separations Corporation, New York,
New York. Bound by A. Horowitz & Sons, Fairfield, New Jersey.
Book Design by Elissa Ichiyasu.

TO MY FATHER:
JACOB DANIEL (1913–1974)

The joy of adventure is unaccountable.
—Agnes Martin

CONTENTS

Gunung Kawi, an ancient Hindu hermitage

FOREWORD

All humans in history have always been born naked, helpless for months, hungry, thirsty, curious, and utterly inexperienced, ergo ignorant. They could not have survived if born where they would freeze, be dehydrated, or burn to death. The most logically propitious place for humans to survive and prosper within our planetary biosphere was on the coral atolls of the South Pacific and North Indian Oceans. Here, the barrier reefs broke up the great seas. The temperature of the almost still water inside the lagoons was so compatible with life that head-above-water humans could stay in them continuously, without any unfavorable effect. The lagoons abounded in fish, and there were mildly sloping, easy-to-walk-in-or-out-upon beaches of white sand. Crystal fresh waters poured down the mountainsides, and coconuts full of milk fell to the ground around the humans. Fruits were plentiful, and there were no wild animals to eat the helpless baby humans.

We know little about the Balinese prior to their island's hundreds of independent village-size kingdoms being militarily overwhelmed by the Dutch in the early seventeenth century. But there are clearly demonstrable cultural clues to be found in the art and folklore relationships existing between the coastal people of southern India and the people of the South Pacific's and Indian Ocean's islands.

In southeast coastal India we find the place called Maha Bali Puram, meaning in our language "the big Balinese city." At Maha Bali Puram we find a large, hill-size unit rock of black granite which has been sculpturally reduced, without in any way fractionating its mass, into a large temple, spaciously and ornately decorated and integrally surrounded by a full-size elephant and other full-size god-animals and gods. On the southwest coast of India, in the complex of islands in greater Bombay harbor, we find another single rock island, known as Elephantis, which this time has been sculpturally hollowed out to leave the insides of a great temple within whose walls are integrally sculptured the same gods and cultural animals as those of Maha Bali Puram. Both of these two—one convex and the other concave—giant, mountain-size sculptural undertakings must have required centuries, and armies of sculptors,

Stone carvings at the Temple of Death, Tampak Siring

to execute. Despite the time, size, and geographical remoteness from one another, they seem to have been conceived and executed in one day by one sculptor.

The sculpturing arts of Bali today are apparently genetically operative. In a new large building in Bali there is a thirty-foot-high by twenty-foot-wide and ten-foot-deep masonry chimney with a total external surface of six thousand square feet. This surface was totally, intricately, and masterfully sculptured by two boys, one fifteen and the other twelve, all in a month's time. They had no drawings to work from. The whole intricate and complex folklore subject patterning seems to have been comprehensively pre-envisioned.

So old and powerful is their culture that the always masterful sculptural capability is evenly operative in all the Balinese. One can take over where the other left off and no difference in the conceiving and the execution is detectable. This gives a false sense of low-cost mass production when applied to small single sculptures of animals and other items, none of which could be sculptured by one in one hundred Europeans.

Quite a number of years ago, my architect friend Lim

Chong Keat secured the site for the building of his house in Ubud, Bali. I went with him to his proposed homesite. We were accompanied by approximately a dozen of the Ubud artists. The artists, carrying machetes, opened up the woods, allowing us to reach the site. The approach went through a deep ravine and up a very steep hillside. As our inspection finished, a torrential rain began, and we hurried down the hill into the dryness of a house. To while away the time, I asked the Balinese artists to use their machetes to cut and bring in a number of bamboo poles, which they then split for me into powerfully stiff sticks, each of them one foot in length. I needed 120 such struts with which to produce a tensegrity sphere. Then I asked them to split some more bamboo even further to make tension lacings. I then made them a four-foot-diameter tensegrity sphere in which none of the compression members touched any other. The whole thing was held together only in tension. This tensegrity sphere was based on the high-frequency triangulated icosahedron, which I've used in all my geodesic dome mathematics. Unintentionally, I had produced for the Balinese something not only deeply intimate to their own experience but innate in their Balinese genes. The Balinese said, "You must have been here long, long ago." They decided that I had been in Bali thousands of years ago. My tensegrity sphere was something that seemed to them to be obviously Balinese. This gave me very special status in Bali.

The rain stopped. Coming out onto the terrace of the house we found that the ravine across whose dry bottom we had walked our way in was now covered with a roaring torrent. Within fifteen minutes the Balinese, wielding their machetes, had cut enough bamboo to produce a strong twenty-foot bridge.

A few years ago, I was asked by a group of Balinese artists to speak to them in Champuan on the outskirts of Ubud. I talked to them about the fear that Bali might be ruined by the rest of the world, and I assured them that I was confident that this would never happen. My reasons were as follows.

The Balinese people form something close to an unbroken human continuum of hundreds of thousands of years of successful life. They are, number one, water people.

Those who have been fortunate enough to be sailors, particularly on sailing ships that go offshore on long voyages, know how quickly everyone not only "knows all the ropes" but knows every last fastening of the ship, knows every weakness and every strength of both ship and its crew, knows all the personalities intimately, knows who can do what best so that when great emergencies occur in hurricane seas, no politicians are necesssary to find jobs for anyone or to tell people what to do. Everyone knows spontaneously what to do, everyone does things coordinatedly, devotedly, swiftly, neatly, effectively. There is such an esprit of cooperation that when one big ship in a storm is just surviving and discovers another ship that is foundering, so vivid is everyone's sense of peril that we find the crew of the first ship going successfully to rescue the crew of the foundering ship, bringing the rescued back aboard their own.

At sea, everyone knows what it's all about; everyone does everything together. Every rope is neatly coiled, not for aesthetic pleasure but so that the ropes will be "free for running" when an emergency comes. All long-time island dwellers who were once boat people treat their island like a boat. They keep their island neat and all its resources "free for running."

All the Balinese know all about everything that goes on in Bali. We find them all going out to the rice fields together; the whole town goes out. We find the whole town going into its music, into its dance, into its ceremonies together, cooperatively, coordinatedly; some play the music while others perform the dances. Everybody does everything together. All do what they do magnificently well.

I made it clear to the Balinese as best I could how it happened that people from around the rest of the world became competitive instead of cooperative. It is difficult to explain Ice Ages to the equatorial Balinese. However, some have now seen machine-made ice cubes. Bali having several active volcanoes, the people are all too familiar with vast lava flows. I pictured to them a world being covered with vast ice-cube flows sometimes over a mile deep. I explained to the Balinese that our planet earth has had four known Ice Ages. They average a million years apiece. The intervals between them average a quarter of a million years. Together, their history covers a known total of four-and-three-quarters million years. The Leakey family's proofs of the presence of humans on our planet for three million years take us back through two Ice Ages and two intervals to the end of the second Ice Age. As an Ice Age develops, more and more of the earth's water is frozen, which greatly lowers the ocean level and reveals previously hidden, interconnecting land masses. At the time of the last Ice Age's occurrence, the sea-hidden, inter-island underwater connections revealed themselves as continental isthmuses and peninsulas. For instance, the great islands of Java, Sumatra, Borneo, the Philippines, Sulewezi, and Bali became integral parts of the Malay Peninsula; New Guinea was part of continental Australia, and so on.

During its formative period, the ice mantle drove the northern continents' fur-skinned wild animals southward into, for instance, the new peninsula-extensions of the Euro-Asiatic mainland. The surprised natives learned gradually to cope with these animals—hunted some, domesticated others such as sheep, pigs, dogs, and goats; and mounted or directed some, such as horses, elephants, and water buffaloes. As the ice withdrew, melting to fill the oceans and seas, the islands became once more isolated but now inhabited with both domesticated and wild animals. Until recently, tigers were found in western Bali.

The great architectural feature of Bali is that of the vertical gap atop the gateways of their walled-in royal dwelling compounds—which gap, the Balinese explain, represents the gap that occurred long ago between once united Bali and Java. This occurred only 30,000 years ago, when the last Ice Age began to melt away and its waters once again separated the islands. Thus, Balinese legend-supported memory goes back 30,000 years.

I told them about the conditions under which, long ago, islanded water people, abandoning their rice paddies, went north, following their sheep and goat herds as the ice melted away. Others did so by living on the hunting of wild animals. Often they found living conditions very difficult. Struggling, they found themselves lethally competitive over occupation of the all too few places that were propitious for their support. Gradually their languages diverged. All this brought about entirely different ways of behaving. It swiftly fostered the "you or me, not enough for both" concept.

I told the Balinese artists about a poet of the northern world, of the world of competition, named Kipling, whose poems make it clear how human beings can exist under the conditions of severe competition and fighting, yet maintain that extraordinary esprit of life.

Kipling was a man who loved life very much, but who as a poet felt very deeply the shortcomings, the frequent injustices of the competitive world. I quoted from him. There was present a great scholar of Balinese, English, and other languages, who had lived in Bali for his whole life. He told me that my Balinese interpreter's translation was the most elegant and eloquent piece of English-into-Balinese interpreting that he had ever known. I quoted Kipling's "L'Envoi":

When Earth's last picture is painted,
And the tubes are all twisted and dried,
The oldest of colors have faded
And the youngest of critics have died,
We shall rest
And well shall we need to
Lie down for an eon or two
'Til the master of all good workmen
Shall put us to work anew.

Then only the master shall praise us,
And only the master shall blame,
No one will work for money,
And no one will work for fame.
But all for the love of the working
And each in his separate star
Shall draw the thing as he sees it
For the God of things as they are.

As I finished reciting, I was astonished, for the Balinese all ran down to me from their surrounding seats, saying, "That's it. *'All for the love of the working.'"*

And that is Bali; it's not the rest of the world. Those who really love the work and love it together and love to support and give happiness to all others are going to out-survive all the selfish competition on our planet.

Ana Daniel is in love with Bali. I, too, am in love with Bali. Therefore I care very much what kind of love people have for Bali. I can say from my experience in Bali that Ana Daniel's love for Bali is the kind with which I hope Bali will always be blessed. Ana has lived intimately with the Balinese, and she writes of them tenderly and knowingly. Behind the Balinese mask she has found "all for the love of the working." All for the love of life as it is.

R. BUCKMINSTER FULLER

Gateway

I Nyoman Kakul

PREFACE

When I went to Bali in 1973 my goal was to photograph Balinese dance theatre. But my passion for art-performance led me to become a student of I Nyoman Kakul. Kakul, a renowned dancer and actor, is one of the last of the great classical Balinese masters. Because of Kakul, I found myself in situations which I might not have sought out otherwise. As Kakul's student I learned and performed ritual Balinese dance, and these experiences changed my understanding of what I saw. Kakul molded my movements, shared his culture and myths with me, revealed a Balinese cosmology expressed in dance, made it possible for me to photograph sacred ritual performance, and ultimately offered a glimpse into the process of personal transformation. *Bali: Behind the Mask* is not intended as an analysis of Balinese dance theatre but is rather the record of a participant.

At the center of the island of Bali stands the Gunung Agung, the Great Mountain of the Ancestors. Gunung Agung is the center of the Balinese universe, and all direction has reference to it. An individual's relative position or orientation is "upward toward the Mountain," on whose heights the gods live, or "downward toward the sea," where all evil spirits dwell in the depths of the unknown. Situated at the border between tropical Asia and the arid southwestern islands, Bali developed a culture that exists at peace amidst converging forces. And because the Balinese observe the past as well as the present, they are connected, through an ancient oral tradition, to their revered ancestors, whose teachings emphasize unity as a central theme. This heightened awareness in the population, developed cooperatively over thousands of years, is facilitated by the extraordinarily entertaining and instructive "mass media." The strength of this oral tradition, communally ritualized in the popular arts, made possible a history of integration that bypassed the violence experienced by other ancient cultures. For the Balinese, art serves as a model for social order. They have metamorphosed foreign philosophies, culture, politics, and religion into distinct Balinese expressions, incorporating new rulers and rituals into native traditions. In his article "Balinese Theatre: Coping with the Old and New" (1980), Richard Wallis illuminates the impact of this attitude. "The processes of recognition, inclusion, and containment of mysterious, threatening, and potentially destructive forces are the essential functions of the two most ancient ritual art-per-formances in Bali: the *Wayang Kulit* [Shadow Puppet theater] and the *Topéng* [Mask theater]."

Kakul reinterpreted ancient teachings into theatre that expressed contemporary themes while remaining true to its traditional forms. But Kakul's capacity to communicate these teachings to an international audience finds its explanation in the very essence of Balinese maintenance of a balanced society, and not in our "discovery" of him.

In Bali, people never do anything in a simple way that they can do in a complex way. Multiple aspects of time, space, economics, and religion have created traditions that operate simultaneously and seem to infuse a gracefulness into every situation.

Balinese concepts of time are different from ours. Several different notions of time, for instance, govern the nature of day-to-day activities, special events, and personal lives. Qualities attributable to these "times" may be cyclic or linear, distant or immediate, sacred or secular, personal or communal. Performance of ritual activity is also related to interlocking calendars. (The Balinese employ several different systems for reckoning the passing of time: an Indian-derived system of twelve lunar months, a Javanese-Balinese system of cycles of various-sized "weeks," and the 365-day system of the Western tradition.)

On an island with limited farmland but an abundance of water, irrigation societies have bound villagers together and with other villages all over the island to form the basis of a sophisticated, highly interdependent, and successful wet-rice agricultural system. The economic structures of Balinese families and villages are fundamentally supported by surplus rice production. The need for cooperation among otherwise unrelated groups of people is emphasized in all the ancient Balinese teachings. Manuscripts from as early as the eighth century A.D. tell of cooperative organizations that governed the use of waters originating from the same source, and since wet-rice farming dates back to the beginning of the first millennium or earlier in Bali, we can assume that these ethics have existed as

an unbroken tradition far longer than those of other cultures exposed to foreign influence.

Balinese villages are laid out with these communal and metaphysical concepts in mind. Each village must have three temples, to which all the villagers "pay dues": the Ancestor Temple, the Community Temple, and the Temple of Death. Inside the villages, intersecting lanes, bound by casings of walls and inner walls, appear to be cosmological mazes. Here, the belief in the cardinal points reveals yet another dimension—the more brittle, vulnerable constructions of this world, where evil spirits may appear at any crossroads. But Balinese consciousness of metaphysical patterns is most powerful during ceremonies or movements of transition: directly behind the portals of family compounds stands a "barrier" wall whose function is to obstruct menacing spirits, known to travel only in straight lines. In cremation ceremonies, one of the most difficult rites of passage, a family must carry the remains of the deceased from the compound to the cremation grounds. The body, carried by family and villagers in a high tower, is taken from the compound in a fevered rush. In this brief but dangerous journey, many intersections must be crossed, and no effort is spared in the erratic, boisterous, and frenzied attempt to "fool" evil spirits lurking at crossroads. The carriers zigzag, turn round and round, run and sprint—unusual behavior in Bali. But the tower is never in peril of falling. After the arrival at the cremation grounds, the family, still fearful that demons may have attached to the deceased's soul, quickly rush the body to a sarcophagus and then onto the pyre. In this way, any remaining evil spirits lingering on the tower will be demolished independently of the release of the soul.

Because the Balinese experience their spirituality as an integral part of their lives, all, from toddlers to the very old, are adept at kicking metaphysical concepts off the backs of their heels. Joking, a common form of communication, is subtle and understated. Balinese jokes mock personal etiquette, satirize societal cadence, and laugh at cosmological consequences. When I performed a headstand, my young friend, four-year-old Wayan, admonished me to be careful and then ran off, laughing uncontrollably. Later his mother explained to me that Wayan had been impressed with the feat but would never do it himself, because the crown of his head, receptive to heaven, would have touched the ground—thereby disrupting a delicate balance within his soul. The next time I saw Wayan, he told me that he admired my bravery but thought I was a little crazy. And if to be accepted is to be teased, the Balinese teach values of trust in a way as complex as their organization of time. Brazen children who ridicule an adult's idiosyncratic behavior are called "naughty," but not with reproach. Everyone shares in the joke, commending the children for their acute observations and encouraging their independent creative thoughts.

The "human will" is seen mainly as a negative force that must be held in check, but suppression of the individual or control of expression is not the Balinese way to balanced life. Instead, overt acknowledgment of and fascination with "Powers of Darkness" account for a vast tradition of purification. Ritual offerings are made both to maintain a thriving cooperative society and as appeasement of evil.

OFFERING

. . . in sacred works, where the acts will not, in themselves, result in anything, but may be rewarded if they please the divinity to whom they are addressed—where, therefore, there can be said to be no direct material purpose—the form is the total statement; and its distinctive quality is that reverent dedication which man brings only to divinity. *The sense of the dedicated act is to serve, not oneself, but the object of one's dedication,* and it is therefore characterized by a quality of selflessness, discipline and even of depersonalization.
—MAYA DEREN
Divine Horsemen

The Balinese are always making offerings: producing ritual objects and using them in religious ceremonies. Making offerings is considered a continual act of devotion. These offerings take many forms—flowers, food, textiles—but their purpose is the same. The Balinese believe that the Supreme Deity, God Who Is All, has given them a splendid bounty; their good fortune cannot be possessed, it can only be tended with thanksgiving offered. Ritual offerings are made privately inside family compounds: deposited haphazardly on the ground, strewn on shrines, on the lanes and roads; and performed publicly and communally at the village temples. In his book *The Art of the Balinese Offering,* David Stuart-Fox states the five aspects of offering or sacrifice: "offerings to the gods, to the demons or those forces that have the power to disturb the orderly running of the universe, to the souls of the dead, to the souls of the living, and to holy persons."

Dance is one of the very special forms of communal offering, and it has a vital function in all Balinese ceremonies. Everyone knows that the gods like to be entertained, and once a celebration is planned, the head of a village arranges for the entertainment with communal funds. The performance begins when the dancers and actors are ready. If unforeseen rain threatens, everyone will wait for an auspicious moment, since for a ceremony to succeed (that is, for the offerings to be accepted by the gods), the performance *must* take place eventually. There's no anxious anticipation or concern, and once I waited six hours for the start of a play. Sometimes, if a dance-drama troupe is especially popular, the actors will schedule several village celebrations, arriving at 1 or 2 a.m. and then perform into the hours past dawn. Our own expectations of a formal, fixed time for beginnings and endings of events, payment for tickets, and possible cancellation are completely absent from this sort of ritual theater. Since membership in communal institutions is part of each villager's life, "payment for entry" doesn't exist. On the contrary, the essence of all offerings is that payment is made to the gods, and the performance is enjoyed by the gods and mortals alike.

Kakul danced in the spirit of offering. Born of a farming family in the village of Batuan in 1905, he was in many ways unique among dancers of Bali. When he was thirteen years old he was already part of a traveling show performing

Kakul (Photograph by Henri Cartier-Bresson, c. 1954)

masked dances of animal spirits; his costumes, made almost entirely from coconut leaves and coconut husk masks, portrayed characters in ancient Balinese mythology. During his travels around the island he studied Baris, a rigorous warrior dance, then learned the ultra-refined Gambúh.

Kakul performed in many villages in his district in the fertile central plains of Bali, and as his reputation spread, he came to be in demand as a teacher as well. He moved continually from district to district, teaching in royal courts and recruiting young dancers and actors from among the local populations. Sometimes he stayed in one village for several years at a time. Kakul became adept in the extensive repertory of Balinese dance-theater forms, culminating his theatrical career by becoming the leader of a five-man Topéng troupe. Set among a grand parade of masked dances, the dramatic Topéng performances provided an arena for the subtleties of his skilled, diverse movements. He totally assumed the characters he portrayed, gaining renown as a comedian as well as a tragedian of sublime artistry.

Kakul was devoted to the sacred traditions of his art. His attitudes of reverence were infused with a sense of dignity. He emphasized character development in all his instructions. He was courageous, poised, dispassionate, and funny. He competed wholeheartedly with other dance troupes, thereby raising the standards of the dance, and he instilled this spirit of competition into his students. Then, by including them in ritual dance ceremonies performed with his troupe, he publicly risked his self-esteem, in typically Balinese manner, by staking his reputation on the students' performance. He thought it most important for women to show their strength and took a stand by teaching young Balinese girls the attitudes of power demonstrated in the Baris. His first female warrior, his daughter Dawan, performed the Baris in the 1950s.

In 1953 Kakul was a member of the Balinese dance troupe that toured major world capitals. When he returned to his native village of Batuan, he purchased several rice paddies and cultivated his own fields along with other farmers in the neighborhood.

During the 1970s Kakul joined tours of Indonesian dancers to Czechoslovakia, Holland, India, the Soviet Union, and West Germany. Westerners sought him out, and he taught them the basics of Balinese dance. Kakul did not rely on verbal explanation to communicate his art. His broad vocabulary of movement and sense of humor became the universal point of contact that attracted and influenced many performing artists from the most progressive theaters of the West.

POKOK

Pokok yeh is a water source or spring. *Pokok kayu* is the living stump of a tree from which new shoots may sprout. *Pokok canalso* refers to the founder of a family, the origins of a village.
—COLIN MCPHEE
Music in Bali

Underlying all artistic form in Bali is an essential connection with the spiritual realm through which ancestral teachings become manifest. *Pokok* is a crucial word in Balinese cosmology. It is homage to origins, roots, and foundations. *Pokok,* as it relates to music, is the skeletal source of instrumentation, harmony, and rhythm. It is the nuclear melody around which all other notes are arranged. In dance, the contact of the dancer's feet on the earth and the alignment of the legs and torso determine the *pokok* stance. The degree of turn-out at the hips and the amount of bending at the knees combine to increase downward pressure on the balls of the feet, intensifying the contact. (In this sense, the turn-out is similar to the posture of the ballet dancer, but with this turn-out, all similarity to ballet ends.)

The body posturing of Balinese dance is not spontaneous or self-expressive. Hieroglyphic stances echo the shape of shadow puppets *(wayang kulit),* which are believed to represent deified ancestor spirits. The myriad attitudes, morals, and personalities of the Balinese pantheon of gods, adopted over

Kakul's daughter, Dawan, as a Baris dancer

the past 2,000 years, are dramatized in the vast dance-theater repertory. These characters, human or animal representations of ancestral ethics, recount the teachings of those who infused themselves and their lives with a spirituality so pure that direct communion with God became a common and revered practice.

Pokok is the essential point of departure for the dance steps themselves, and so for the entire alignment of the body in its symbolic posturing. Without the *pokok* stance, connection with ancestral origins is impossible and the spiritual nature of dance cannot be expressed. This basic attitude—one of supreme trust and humility—gives all form in Bali its meaning.

When I began to study with Kakul, he selected the Baris for me to perform. Baris dancers demonstrate both the sacred postures of the warrior of Eastern traditions and the martial arts origins of the dance itself. The Baris emphasizes facial expression, emotional range, and control. It is the basic preparation for and introduction to the dances of Topéng and the theater of transformation. In the training of the Balinese actor, Baris *is pokok*, and Kakul instilled the *pokok* stance as the foundation stone of his teaching. He always stressed *pokok* as the source of expression and the strength from which all movement sprang. He refused to teach the angular position of arms or minute turns of the hands and fingers until this basic posturing was firmly rooted.

Other dance movements and gestures are codified in *lontar* manuscripts, which have been reinterpreted by the Balinese since ancient times. Considering the sacred function of traditional Balinese dance, it seems fairly certain that many of the hand gestures evolved from *mudras* performed by Buddhist and Hindu priests who came to Bali as early as the eighth century A.D. Naya Sari, a Baris posture of resoluteness and completion, reflects the esoteric meaning of the number 9 in Balinese metaphysics (the four cardinal points plus four points in between plus center). The pose emblazoned on sanctuaries all over the island is the manifestation of Sanghyang Widhi, the Supreme Deity. My purpose in raising the issue of esoteric religious symbolism is not to attempt to explain it, but to acknowledge it as the accepted source of dance among all Balinese.

Much theoretical and documentary work already exists on the methods and techniques of Balinese dance instruction. Gregory Bateson and Margaret Mead, in their seminal work on visual and kinaesthetic learning, *Balinese Character: A Photographic Analysis* (1942), documented the work of Mario, a famous Balinese choreographer and dancer, during the 1930s. In this photographic, anthropological study, the first ever done, Bateson and Mead developed a theory of character formation by observing and documenting posture, movement, and facial expression. Their records showed Mario to be such an authoritative, yet intimate, teacher that the question of the students' "will" was dismissed. Their observation of a "disassociatedness of limbs" led Bateson and Mead to conclude that the Balinese dance student learns submission and passivity. My own experience as Kakul's student revealed to me that the more subtle relationships of the eyes to the hands, the feet to the torso, and the breath to the movement are directly communicated from the body of the teacher to that of the student with a more transcendental purpose in mind. The dancer is initiated into a spiritual practice. What is taught is receptivity.

TOPÉNG

Kakul becomes what he plays. For a time, within the mask of Sidha Karya that he is privileged to wear, he functionally *is* the "priest of *dharma*," emissary from the gods and intercessor for mankind.
—JOHN EMIGH
"Mask Theater of Bali"

The Topéng actor is responsible for bringing the past into present time—for animating the ancient doctrines of gods and ancestors with a "special vocabulary of movement." Not only must these divisions of the world of the past and the present be dynamic, but the actor must be adept in the use of humor to shatter the boundaries between the two worlds.

Richard Wallis explores the function of the Balinese actor: "Perhaps we may view Balinese theatre as one way in which people keep conflicting worlds in perspective. Dramatic form and content handle simultaneously both the traditional world of contemporary audiences (of any period) and rationalized worlds depicting highly abstracted times and places from the Balinese literary heritage. Always the audience sees itself (in the attendant stage figures) successfully coping with, and mediating between, both worlds. When aspects of modernization do confront the Balinese, they often resort to theatrical means to neutralize resulting inconsistencies."

Not a great deal is known about the history of Topéng in Bali. Documentation of performances and teachings of this tradition is scant, although ancient manuscripts and stone relief carvings have shown that the holy ritual Topéng performances, especially those of pre-Hindu communities around the crater of the Gunung Agung, view the mask as an actual manifestation of divine power. These masks, used in the worship of ancestors, the original Red, Yellow, and Brown Men, represent the Man of Fire, the Man of the Coconut, and the Man of the Earth, respectively. During the eighth and ninth centuries, wandering priests used the mask in theater performances to communicate the teachings of the Buddha. An edict of the king who reigned during this time states: "It is through the mask of the Holy Man Kenakamuni that the doctrine of religion will be spread. Thus, the Topéng performance will always be related with the spiritual realm." And further stated in this *lontar*, "the only information transmitted through this Topéng should concern the unity of religious doctrines"—in this case the unification of Buddha and Shiwa.

Storytelling, the main course of Topéng dance theater, further extends the educational function of Topéng. The *Chronicles of the Kings*, part of the oral tradition and etched on *lontars* since the sixteenth century, constitute the source material of the dramatic Topéng "art-performance." By telling and retelling the histories of these dynasties, the Balinese have come to

know their ancestors, and to strengthen their commitments to, and belief in, their teachings. Communities build shrines to demarcate holy places for the purpose of ancestor worship, and celebration of these shrines affords occasion for perpetual illumination of their ethics.

Actors of the Topéng "art-performance" frequently come from society at large. These dancers have always enjoyed a special position—within their inherent connection with the general public is the potential to transform their theater into an effective tool for interpreting the strongest secular issues. At the beginning of the twentieth century, Topéng was often used as a form of political communication between the kings of Bali, and many of the dancers were arrested for criticizing the Dutch government of that time. Repression also occurred during the Japanese occupation of Bali in the Second World War.

People in Bali go to see Topéng dance-theater again and again because the interpretation of ancient stories always changes. A fundamental connection with the ancestors is maintained and contemporary life is given a meaningful context. Improvisation and satire enliven the communication. Information and devotion are renewed. Artists deepen their own understanding, and the population learns the values conveyed through Topéng stories.

Kakul introduced me to Bali's ritual art of transformation. As a virtuoso Topéng artist, Kakul achieved his most acclaimed performance in the Topéng Pajegan, or sacred Topéng solo. In these potentially dangerous portrayals, during which one actor wears a myriad of masks in rapid succession, Kakul embodied the universe. He was called upon to act, as well as to move, in a trance. The final mask of this ritual, Sidha Karya, incorporates the demonic element of trance with the sacred functions of the priest. The responsibility of transmitting the offerings (necessary to successfully complete the ceremony) to the gods and the bestowal of blessing from the gods onto the community are mediated not by a priest—but by

Kakul, the Topéng dancer. At the end of the performance, Kakul transforms from Sidha Karya to the Pengejuken. He grabs a child in the audience and bestows food upon him from the offerings of Sidha Karya. The child is frightened yet excited to be chosen to receive this blessing. As the One Who Takes Up People in His Arms, Kakul is the manifestation of evil grabbing at good, enticing and threatening, and it is his responsibility to honor as well as to disarm evil.

When Kakul and I first met, I suppose that I was perceived as a potentially destructive force, threatening with my camera at every turn. Kakul dispelled the threat by revealing the humorous nature of my documentation. He included me in his troupe. He made it possible for me to laugh at myself and at the same time accept the trust extended to me by the Balinese with whom I lived. Kakul's openness to a spiritual source, his devotion to the teachings of a high Hindu priest, and his knowledge of the classical Balinese dances made his contribution as a choreographer and actor all the more significant. My photographic and written records of Kakul's instructions do not represent the definitive techniques of Balinese dance but attempt to show the way of one particular master.

Balinese dance-theater is not about the fleeting gesture. Even to the Balinese themselves, who are constantly involved in the execution of minute, well-defined rituals, the meanings and interpretations of their actions are often points of conjecture; but, more usually, they are simply explained as ancestral teachings, custom, gossip, or as having entirely mysterious and sacred origins. And so my own gathering of information and photography of Balinese rituals and dance—my offering—is colored by my daily life with the Balinese people—that is, by conjecture, ancestral teachings, custom, gossip, and experiences of entirely mysterious origins. I have not attempted to show the never-before-seen wonders of this island but, rather, to illuminate the kinds of relationships that emerge from the ways of Balinese life.

ANA DANIEL

BALI

BEHIND THE MASK

THE YELLOW BUTTERFLY

A story is told about a very bad man who stole from everyone in his village. All his neighbors chased after him yelling threats and curses, and finally ran him out of the village. Being terribly frightened, the man hid under a big tree in the graveyard, and after hiding there for a long time, quiet and still, he began a meditation to God.

A few days passed before the Spirit of the Tree interrupted his meditation.

"Alas, O Man, why have you been sitting here for so long?"

The man did not answer, assuming that the voice was a disturbance of the thoughts in his heart. He continued his meditation until, on the day of the full moon, the Spirit of the Tree interrupted him once more.

"Alas, O Man, why are you still here? Go away from here!"

"Who is speaking?" the man asked, now very startled. "Are you the owner of the graveyard? Or are you the God of the Night? Or are you the God Who Is All?"

"I am the Spirit of This Wood and the Keeper of This Place. I bid you to leave immediately."

"You can't tell me to leave here," the man countered. "Don't you know that this graveyard is for us all; that from here we'll all go Home forever?"

The Spirit of the Tree reassured him. "Of course this place is for everybody, but first you must be dead. Those who still live must return to their homes. I implore you to leave at once!"

Suddenly a white temple pigeon landed on the branches of the Tree. The man listened to the mild cooings of the bird and asked the Tree Spirit, "There, O Tree, the sacred Titiran is sitting on your branches, and I cannot understand what it says. Please, can you tell me?"

The Tree Spirit explained the meaning of the Titiran's words to the man: "Don't kill this man. He has been a thief who stole from everyone and the people of his village ran after him. That is the reason for his hiding. So I beg of you, O Tree Spirit, please help this man."

After sharing the message of the Titiran, the Tree Spirit roared with laughter. "Have you heard that, Man? Is it true that you were a Bad Man? And that the people of the village chased you out? And that now you want to meet God? Is this true, Man? Is this really true, Man?"

The man answered with great embarrassment, "O Tree Spirit, yes, it is all true. Can you help me in my search to meet God, or can you come to my aid so that I may live safely in this world?"

"Alas," the Tree Spirit responded, "it will be very difficult for you to live safely in the world because all the people of your village are after you. And now nobody wants to be with you. I have a better idea. You will go to the palace of Batara Yama di Pati. That way, you will not be killed by your angry neighbors. It will benefit you to live there and be a servant of Batara Yama di Pati, the Mighty Keeper of Dead Souls."

"How will I get there?"

"I will give you a special carriage."

"But I don't understand. What kind of carriage can you give me? Where is it? Anyway, what road would I take?"

"Be patient! I really will give you a carriage that will take you to the palace of Batara Yama de Pati."

Then the Tree Spirit made two Yellow Butterflies appear in front of the man, one large and one small. The man was astonished and asked, "How can I sit on the backs of these very small creatures?"

"Be patient!" insisted the Tree Spirit.

Then the Tree Spirit withdrew into a deep meditation and magically the butterflies grew larger until the man was able to sit comfortably on the back of the larger creature.

"You will sit on the Large Yellow Butterfly on your journey to the palace, and the Small Yellow Butterfly will serve as your guide. But you must always remember," cautioned the Tree Spirit, "throughout this journey, you must not speak even a single word."

The man climbed on the back of the Large Butterfly and immediately began to feel very very good. He began to feel as if he himself were the butterfly. The man thanked the Tree Spirit, and the Tree Spirit said, "You are welcome, Man. May you arrive in the palace quickly and safely."

The Small Butterfly led the way. They began their ascent into the skies, and soon they were over the open seas. So amazed by the vastness of the ocean below that he completely forgot himself, the

 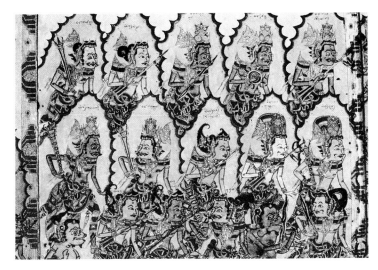

man exclaimed, "Béh, how could I have known!"

Suddenly the Large Butterfly plummeted toward the water but managed a graceful landing that left them both afloat.

Meanwhile, the Small Butterfly, which was still in the skies leading the way, turned and did not see its friend following behind. It looked all around, and was surprised to see them floating on the waters below. It flew down to them and began scolding the man.

"Stupid Man, you were forbidden to speak while we were in flight!"

Meanwhile, the Tree Spirit, still deep in meditation, knew of the entire incident and magically gave the Large Butterfly the strength to continue its journey.

After much time over the open seas, the three travelers came to a small island. They spotted a garden in the middle of the island and landed next to a pond in the center of the garden and rested there.

The Small Yellow Butterfly decided to bathe in the pond. As soon as it immersed itself in the water, it turned into a beautiful maiden, and her name was Si Kuning. When the man saw the transformation, he fell deeply in love with the maiden and began to think, How could the palace of Batara Yama di Pati be any more wondrous than this? Maybe God sent this maiden to me and wants me to marry her!

Suddenly, he himself was transformed into a Good Man in the eyes of heaven, and his name was Si Putih. Si Kuning recognized his goodness and fell deeply in love with him. The man then asked the maiden, "Will you accept my love?"

And she answered, "Yes."

"Let us ask for a sign."

They were answered by the Great Voice of the God Siwa, who called down from the heavens, "O Man and Woman, of course I give you my permission to be married. I tell you now, go and bathe in the western spring and from there continue your flight to heaven together. When you arrive at the palace, you will become servants of Batara Yama di Pati, the Mighty Keeper of Dead Souls."

They followed the instructions, and before long arrived at the

inner temple of Batara Yama di Pati. In this temple there were seven maidens, who became upset because they were suddenly aware of an offensive smell. They complained to Batara Yama di Pati with great indignation.

"How can it be that we smell earthly mortals here?"

Batara Yama di Pati came into the palace and called out, "O earthly beings, if you do not reveal yourselves to me, I will be forced to devise a test to expose you."

No one answered.

Batara Yama di Pati then erected a bridge and called out, "Everyone must cross over this bridge. All beings from my kingdom are assured passage, but earthly beings are destined to fall."

And with this command, all the residents of the palace began to cross over the bridge.

In the middle of this trial, the Great Voice of the God Siwa called out: "O Batara Yama di Pati, the Mighty Keeper of Dead Souls, of course there are two mortals who have come from earth. But they have received my permission."

At that moment, the Man and the Yellow Butterfly Maiden fell from the bridge, and Batara Yama di Pati roared with laughter and asked them, "Why have you come here?"

"We are here to seek employment," answered Si Putih and Si Kuning.

"What kind of work can you do?"

"We can do anything, O Mighty Keeper of Dead Souls."

"Can you dance and play music?"

"Yes, I know how to dance and play music," said Si Putih.

Very pleased with the mortal's reply, Batara Yama di Pati commanded Si Putih to instruct all the palace maidens in the ways of the performing arts, and he further said to them all, "Whoever among you can dance the best, I will appoint as Dance Master."

Si Putih began his instructions, teaching every day and night, much to the pleasure of Batara Yama di Pati. But it was Si Kuning who was the finest dancer and was appointed Dance Master by Batara Yama di Pati. They formed a dance troupe and entertained in the palace night and day. To show his appreciation, Batara Yama di Pati, the Mighty Keeper of Dead Souls, changed Si Putih's name to Singha Mega and appointed him leader of all art-performances in the palace.

One day, Batara Yama di Pati advised Singha Mega to take the art-performance troupe and entertain in the palace of the God Indra.

After the performance, the God Indra was so elated that he asked Singha Mega to deliver the following request: "O Batara Yama di Pati, Mighty Keeper of Dead Souls, I would be so honored if your troupe would come to entertain again in my court. I invite you to join with us, and offer my house to you in good faith."

Batara Yama di Pati accepted the invitation and went to the court of the God Indra. The God Indra, especially pleased with the beauty of the music and dance, gave a Jewel to Batara Yama di Pati as a sign of appreciation. Batara Yama di Pati and the art-performance troupe returned to their home and, upon arrival, Singha Mega challenged Batara Yama di Pati, saying, "Since I am the leader of the troupe, I should receive possession of the Jewel."

Batara Yama di Pati, Mighty Keeper of Dead Souls, was outraged by this challenge.

"What impudence! Everything in heaven belongs to me!"

A violent quarrel ensued, which was judged by the God Siwa, Singha Mega's guardian. Finally, the God Siwa called the dispute to an end and declared Singha Mega to be the winner. The opponents agreed to the judgment, and Singha Mega was awarded the Jewel. Furthermore, Batara Yama di Pati appointed Singha Mega the Honored Illuminator of all new arrivals to his palace.

When Singha Mega had painted the impressions of 178 souls, he audaciously freed them to reincarnate before their appointed time. Batara Yama di Pati was angered, and as the freed souls were reincarnating, he caught them, one by an ankle, another by an arm, and caused them to be crippled. Then, as punishment, he forced Singha Mega to reincarnate with his wife Si Kuning—he to become the Puppeteer Who Does Not Speak, and she to become the One Who Accompanies the Performance in Song.

Singha Mega was allowed to take the many kinds of soul paintings with him when he reincarnated to the earth. These images became the wayangs, which he used in performance of the shadow puppet plays, thus teaching to earthly beings the doctrines of God.

EMPTY TIME

Outside the parking lot of the airport in Bali, several *bémos* waited for passengers. The usual fare to the central station was a hundred rupiahs, but the money-taker, who traveled with the driver, tried to make extra fares from the meek and naïve. This included anybody who lived outside his village, and since I was an obvious candidate, the money-taker took my arm and led me to his *bémo*, telling me all the time that I should "charter" the entire vehicle for myself.

"Only five thousand rups," he said. In United States money this was equal to twelve dollars. I made known that five thousand rupiahs was much too expensive by shaking my head and walking away. He charged after me, yelling, "O.K., O.K., O.K.!" and signaled that his price was now only four thousand rups. I laughed at his counteroffer and indicated that it was still too much by bringing my hand to my mouth in imitation of eating. I shrugged my shoulders, offered two thousand rups, and walked away again.

"Listen!" he yelled, motioning for me to come back. "As long as there's rice in the fields, you'll eat; but O.K. Where do you go?" I told him the name of the village, and he said,

"Good, very far, but for you, only three thousand rups. I'll take you there directly, not even one stop."

It was late afternoon. *Bémos* were not numerous near the airport, and my destination, the village of Peliatan, was forty kilometers away. The price was still way out of line, but I agreed because I wanted to get settled by nighttime.

The sun was descending as the *bémo* departed from the airport. The driver made several stops along the fifteen-foot-wide road to pick up passengers in spite of the exclusive-charter bid. At several points, bales of harvested rice lined both sides of the narrow road. Rice fields spread out as far as I could see.

After a stop for refueling near the main terminal, the *bémo* lunged back on the main road that led north toward Peliatan. Several kilometers past the city limits, the road began to swerve, dip, and rise, guided by the terrain of the terraced fields. On each side the paddies disappeared and reappeared, always carved out of hillsides in intricate, abstract patterns. The colors melted in and out of one another: lush dark-green paddies nestled close to the edge of the brown-black earth. Water circulated from field to field, linking one to another.

Hillsides became spectrums of harvest, undulating in progressive rhythms of bronze, hazel, yellow, and amber.

The land descended in gradual terraces until the sheer walls of a ravine dropped into a river forty feet below the road. A work crew lifted heavy boulders from the edge of the river. Men and women worked side by side. In assembly-line manner, they passed enormous stones from the rushing water onto the land, and up the hill, and then braced the boulders against the incline of earth. Women worked in tightly wrapped batik sarongs—wet and clinging, yet not cumbersome. A second crew of women shoveling asphalt off a truck blocked traffic across a rickety old bridge.

The driver stopped and, turning around, motioned to the activity ahead on the road. "New," he said. *"Bagus."* He pointed with pride to the bags of cement.

The money-taker elaborated: the existing wooden bridge was being replaced by a wide concrete structure capable of supporting enormous tourist buses. This new mammoth structure would be wide enough for two *bémos* to pass at the same time, whereas now traffic in only one direction at a time was possible. He also said that motorcycles owned by rich "modern" Balinese would benefit, although he showed some uneasiness about the noisy speeding bikers.

"No good . . . evil spirits. They race through intersections inviting collision."

The women had finished shoveling asphalt from the truck and were now settled at the edge of the road smoking cigarettes and chewing betel nut. Passage was clear, and the driver proceeded across several planks that constituted the remainder of the old bridge. Once on the other side, the money-taker hopped off the *bémo* and deposited some minuscule baskets of flowers at the foot of a statue, which, with a large club, was the Protecting Spirit of the bridge. Having made the offerings necessary to appease malevolent spirits lurking at this juncture, he hopped back on the vehicle and we were again on the road.

The road traced the paddies from open field to village edge, and the *bémo* swerved past eight-foot-high mud walls that gave way to occasional entries. A child and dog appeared, followed by an older child carrying a baby on his hip. An old man, framed by the mud wall, squatted on his threshold watching the activity on the road. We passed several food stands in the center of the village; then the road curved once again, plunging the *bémo* back between the rice fields. The sequence repeated eight or nine times, the road turning north, then northeast, always facing the Gunung Agung at the east central part of the island. This volcanic mountain is, in fact, 160 kilometers north of Denpasar, the main city, but its scale and relationship to the entire island alludes to another standard of measurement. As we traveled, perspectives altered so radically with each turn in the road that on occasion the crater appeared just ahead, looming as if impact were imminent, then abruptly receded into the distance across an expanse of fields, then reappeared as yet another image of deceptive accessibility. At each turn the sun cast longer shadows, creating a final illusion of distance.

After an alarming bend and near collision with a villager who was herding a flock of quacking ducks in the middle of the road, we arrived at Peliatan. The driver jammed on the brakes and stopped abruptly in front of a sign that read "KETUT'S HOMESTAY." There was an arrow on the sign pointing down a footpath that disappeared into a maze of jungle lanes. By the time I got out of the *bémo,* the luggage had already been neatly deposited under the sign and the money-taker was casually waiting to collect his fare. When the business was negotiated, he leaped onto the already speeding vehicle, which had turned daringly around in front of the blind bend in the road, and they were off and out of sight before I began my approach to the "HOMESTAY."

All recognizable signs of the modern world disappeared with my first step onto the footpath. Mud walls on either side enclosed compounds of geometrically arranged structures varying in sophistication from woven palm branches, casually supported by a bamboo superstructure on earth floors, to brick houses, plastered in dense white with red ceramic roofs and glazed Chinese floor tiles. Several people sitting on a tiny pavilion in the first compound ignored my intrusion. They sipped coffee in postures of serene repose as ducks roamed around the courtyard. I continued down the lane past other entrances and finally arrived at Ketut's family compound.

Ketut and two young boys sat cross-legged on a porch. No one noticed me. They were all intently preoccupied with the task of removing a small object from a container and suspending this object from a string attached to the bottom of a kerosene lamp. As I approached, I saw that the objects were spinning and buzzing, and I realized that whatever they were, they had wings and were alive. I was almost on the steps of the porch when Ketut looked up and giggled as if he had been tickled by one of the winged creatures. He carefully but rapidly handed it to one of the boys, and rose to greet me. He was middle-aged, and his countenance was bright and vigorous.

"Hello, hello," he said, pumping my hand. He led me toward a *balé* across the courtyard, which was elegantly furnished with spotted bamboo chairs and flowering orchids. He asked one of the boys to lift my bags off the dirt, and sent the other, who had already put away the winged creature, to the kitchen to fix coffee. We sat down. Ketut offered me a *kretek* cigarette and lit one for himself. The aroma of clove and fresh-brewed *kopi* filled the air. Finally, after everything was arranged for conversation, he asked in Indonesian, "Where are you coming from?"

I said that I had just arrived from California. Ketut smiled and asked, "Oh, you *menari?*" He made dance gestures with

his elegant hands. Apparently, my mime teacher, Leonard Pitt, had already settled into his dance studies and Ketut assumed that I would be doing the same. I said that I also made photographs, and pointed to my camera. Ketut exclaimed, "Portrait, portrait," and showed me photographs that other guests had taken of him. He flipped through the book, which also contained press clippings of reviews from Germany, Boston, and other "exotic" places where his paintings had been exhibited. I was astonished by the two-inch-long thumbnail of his right hand, which he used to turn pages. Ketut noticed my surprise.

"I'm an artist," he said. "I seldom work in the fields. But of course, during large harvests everybody in the *banjar* pitches in." His position in the neighborhood organization gave Ketut status, but, he continued, "I actually do a lot of manual labor. In fact, I lost this nail several times during the construction of the cinema. But painting, my main work, is the way I express devotion to the teachings of our ancestors."

One of the youngsters arrived with *kopi* and more cigarettes.

I asked if Leonard was staying at Ketut's homestay; Ketut said that he lodged at the palace of the village Prince, the Puri Agung.

"Everyone in Peliatan knows Leonard and all about his activities in Bali," Ketut said. "Everybody knows everybody's business here. Even if no one knows for certain, they still know about gossip. You must be very discreet if you plan to live alone. Villagers tell stories about evil spirits who prowl at the edge of the rice paddies, preying on the fears of frail young women alone at night—especially on moonless nights. We've all heard the wailing and moaning of the *leyaks* and are very cautious not to attract their attention."

With this information clearly expressed, Ketut finished his *kretek,* put the lid on his *kopi* glass, and asked if I had already bathed. When I said that I hadn't, Ketut prepared to take me to the *pondoks,* which served as lodging for visitors.

Interior of a family compound

As we left the compound, he asked the boys—his nephews, about six or seven years old—to carry the bags. They cheerfully agreed, and we all walked out of the compound to the end of one lane and turned, after several meters, onto another. A labyrinth of mud walls enclosed the households and outlined the path that jagged for several hundred meters before it opened into a garden at the edge of the rice paddies. The lane shrank to a mere footpath that meandered through the garden past two *pondoks,* woven bamboo and thatched havens. It continued around a lotus pond, past another *pondok* and a well, and finally ended on the far side of a second pond bursting with pink Mandarin lotus blossoms. Here, at the end of the footpath, was my *pondok.* Nestled against a bamboo grove, it faced south onto an expanse of paddies that bordered the village of Mas several kilometers away. To the west a small irrigation stream and more paddies continued a hundred meters down a river canyon and up the opposite bank to the terraced fields of the neighboring village of Pengosekan. Shades of deep red had already touched the tops of the palm trees and the sun was diving toward the horizon as the boys carefully placed the bags on the porch. They fled in a tizzy of laughter and returned, very composed and diligent, carrying the bed linen. The smaller boy, named Madé, lit kerosene lamps on the porch and wished me *"selamat tidur"* with *"mimpi manis."*

Inside the sleeping area, I sat down at a desk next to the window that overlooked the rice fields and lotus pond. Fireflies glowed in the dark rice paddies. The frogs and geckos began an evening concert. I was ready for sweet dreams—stretching the day out, loosening shoulders and neck, extending arms as if they were antennae—when suddenly a huge praying mantis lunged at my armpit and hit its mark with exact aim.

Man weaving a bamboo wall

At dawn, from every direction, the roosters crowed.

A crew of four women and five men were on their way to work in the paddies. The women carried baskets on their heads and small hand knives in the waists of their sarongs. The blade of each knife was a sharpened crescent made from a piece of flat metal; the other side was covered by a wooden handle. This design enabled its user to cut the rice stalks with a swift rotary movement of the wrist while gathering and bundling with the free hand. The rice sheaves, bound as they became too large to handle, were lined up on the edge of the paddies as the day's work progressed. Then they were stacked next to one another, forming a super bundle that was hoisted on top of the basket and carried from the fields on the women's heads.

Men carried sickles, which they also tucked into their sarongs, usually at the small of their backs. Those who were not harvesting rice worked in the paddies that had already been reaped, slashing the dry stalks down in irregular patterns and flinging them onto a stack that grew continually. Finally, the stalks were bundled together, carried off into the village, and spread out on top of the mud walls as protection against monsoons. The stubble that remained in the earth was burned, and then the paddy was flooded.

This particular crew passing through the dawn-streaked sunlight of the bamboo grove just behind my *pondok* was very vocal and humorous. Their voices, soft in the distance, grew more audible as they approached, becoming distinct laughter and storytelling. One voice, full of modulations and gasps, told a long tale that was occasionally interrupted by embellishments from other members of the group, and by continual rounds of laughter from everyone. There was only a momentary pause after a joke before someone else continued with

Irrigation stream

another story. In animated procession they emerged on the south side of the bamboo grove. They climbed onto the paddy ledge on the other side of the wall directly in front of my *pondok* and dispersed into the open fields.

Gentle amorous chidings of the ducks swimming in the irrigation stream replaced the workers' lighthearted chatter. Down the path in the garden an old woman cleared dead leaves from the banana trees. She moved around the small grove, cutting away the shabby growth with efficient strokes until the trees stood in their pristine and uncluttered beauty. Then she took a long stiff whisk broom in hand and swept the remaining debris, revealing the meticulous arrangements of the garden. Her arm firmly grasping the broom, rhythmically swinging from one side to the other, she continued sweeping onto the winding path, clearing the accumulation of the day's rubbish. Drawing curves on the earth, she wound her way through the garden. Finally, completing her work in front of my porch, she looked at me with a full smile of betel-stained teeth, and began a dance that vaguely resembled the "bump"—unabashedly seductive, yet delicately supple. Her head bobbed from left to right; her neck was erect yet loose; her eyes darted to either side. In the midst of these movements, she had turned her whole body with minute and delicate steps, and was now confronting me with her back. The broom still firmly grasped in one hand, she dipped her other arm toward her body and then, flicking the wrist, she soared away from me. She stopped momentarily, just long enough to wiggle her rear end several times. Then another flick of the wrist took her lilting into more steps that led to yet another pose—motionless, except for her swinging rear end. She dissolved into laughter halfway down the path, then continued boom-booming on out of the garden, broom still in hand, past the patterned ribbon of dirt that connected the garden to the village lanes.

I followed and caught up with her, trying to mimic her dance; occasionally she would bump into my back, breaking into more laughter. She went as far as Ketut's compound and disappeared into the kitchen.

That morning, the courtyard was filled with huge woven grass mats that supported row after row of *jaja*. The round flat cookies, which would be used for ceremonial offerings, were made of black and white rice: the black rice had been rolled into a mandala-like design in the center of a white rice dough. Ibu, Ketut's wife, was cutting thin slices from the "rice log," which she carried to the mats for drying. The morning sun was bright and several of the *jaja* were already crisp. Ibu gathered several cookies onto a plate and took them, with a glass of *kopi*, to Ketut, who was grooming his pet crickets. Ketut seemed a little bleary.

"Oh," he moaned, "I haven't been able to get a decent night's sleep for a week. All over Bali, people are preparing to cremate the bones of their ancestors." He spoke quickly, almost distractedly, not permitting any interruption. "These cremations must be completed before the Eka Dasa Rudra, a once-in-every-hundred-years celebration that will take place next year. *Aduh!* Things will be *ramai* indeed! In Peliatan alone, fifty families, including my wife's family, will be making arrangements and I'm sure that this is going to be my last free day before the work really begins in earnest."

Ketut sipped his coffee casually, but I could see that he was agitated. He inserted a minuscule plumed grass sheaf into one of the cricket cages, twirling the stick between the forefinger and thumb—the one with the elegant nail—of his right hand.

"Sincerity and attention determine the merit of the offering," he said pensively. "*Halus.* We've already consulted with the priests who know which offerings are necessary for the souls of the dead. Ibu will arrange the offerings according to the priests' instructions, and as an artist, I have the responsibility of making the sarcophagus. Then, when everything is ready, the family will unearth the bones. A high priest will bless the bones many times before they are placed in the high tower and carried to the Pura Dalem on the appointed day. Finally, we'll transfer the bones into the Singha sarcophagus, which will be burned on the cremation pyre."

Ketut paused, assuming that I did not understand.

"The auspicious nature of the Eka Dasa Rudra will require many special offerings. First of all, the cremations will begin to purify the earth. The souls who are still bound down must be released into a higher realm of existence, and our offerings will ensure a welcome passage."

As he talked, Ketut moved the tickle stick from cage to cage. After completing this agitation, he removed the lid from the end of one of the cages and carefully enveloped the creature within his hands. Then, unfolding them slowly, he displayed a huge shiny cricket. "This is my prize fighting cricket," he said. "Notice how smooth and silky its wings are." He slipped his elegant thumbnail under the cricket's wings, holding the creature gently and securely within his left hand. "This one is as strong as a beast and will surely win several rounds for me at today's match."

In a nearby *banjar,* he told me, the men had arranged fighting matches every three days during the "season." "Since the season is now coming to an end, the strongest fighters will be there. I'm up against a tough contest, but this cricket gives me great confidence."

Ketut cupped his hands around the cricket and released it into its cage. He put aside his *kopi* and, with ritual care, he covered each cage with a curved bamboo lid, securing them in a box with a carved base. He then carefully wrapped the box with a very large spotless white cloth. Ketut explained that because this beautiful box was a family heirloom that had been handed down from his grandfather, the crickets kept in it were endowed with an unusual spirit and zeal.

It was well before the beginning of the midday match, but Ketut was very eager to leave, as the walk through the paddies would take considerable time.

In front of the *balé banjar,* some boys and girls were snaring dragonflies with thin wooden darts attached to eight-foot bamboo rods. The children stood poised under the hovering flock, carefully watching the movement of each insect, anticipating a brief hesitation—then, with great precision and a swift flick of the wrist, one child zapped a huge fly with the thin weapon and sent it falling to the ground. The children caught many flies in a few minutes' time, collected their prizes in woven bags, and ran toward the river gully to try their bait on the frogs lurking by the edge of the water.

We left the main road and walked down a small footpath that went through a bamboo grove. Ketut led the way, which seemed to follow the exact path taken by the early morning workers, and sure enough, it passed in front of my *pondok* and continued out into the rice fields. We walked on a narrow ledge that bordered the paddies and a small irrigation stream. This ledge went on for several hundred meters before the main irrigation canal for Peliatan's southernmost fields intersected it and created several tributary streams. Ketut removed his sandals and picked up the bottom edges of his sarong. He stepped into the canal, delicately glided to the other side, where he swirled each foot at the water's edge to remove any excess dirt, and slipped on his sandals without missing a step in his established pace. He stepped up onto another ledge, which was bordered by two *sawahs,* and proceeded toward the village of Mas. A flock of satisfied ducks floated on one field, feeding on the scant remains of the harvest.

Immediately ahead, several farmers were lounging inside a tiny *pondok,* enjoying protection from the hot midday sun. Ketut waved hello. Apparently one of the men found Ketut's parcel comical and yelled back a funny remark, which sent the others into titters and barely containable laughter. Ketut seemed rather embarrassed, but took the joke lightly and explained, ''They know I'm addicted to the cricket matches. I've taken this exact route for so many seasons that people have come to know the purpose of my trek. That one man said, 'So this is how my labor in the fields ends—as cricket feed!' '' Ketut chuckled. ''Balinese rice is the most beautiful and the most nutritious. It makes perfect sense that our prize fighters should also eat it. But nutrition isn't everything. There are other qualities that have to be developed. Of course I'm referring to a tough and ferocious character! So it doesn't hurt to drop whiskey onto the rice. I even have a pulverized blend of ivory, dried roast suckling pig, and gold leaf that will endow the creatures with still more sublime attributes. It may all seem very extravagant to you, but the quantity is so minute that several grams will last my entire life.'' He shrugged his shoulders and stopped momentarily to light a *kretek.* The path dissolved into a maze.

''I've walked through these paddies all my life and have never been lost,'' Ketut said reassuringly. ''We'll continue 'toward the sea' for several kilometers more.''

The ledge became mud steps and descended to another field, then descended two more *sawahs* in the same manner until it reached the edge of the river gully. Ketut walked steadfastly down the steps past each succeeding paddy, leaving sight of the Gunung Agung behind as he proceeded into the terraced hillside.

The sacred mountain Gunung Agung

The only visible signs of rice that remained were the Cilis, which stood at the head of each empty *sawah*. These Cilis, fertility goddesses made of bundles of harvested rice, were placed with grains hung toward the earth, body and crown fashioned from the long yellow stalks. Proof of the successful harvest was evident in the tiny woven trays laden with flowers and burnt-incense attached to the poles supporing the Cilis.

From these reaped fields, the path turned and climbed the terraces owned by the village of Mas. A small brick shrine, marked in the landscape by a blooming frangipani tree, stood by a trickling spring that ran into the main river, whose waters were used by both Peliatan and Mas. Ketut said he knew all the villagers whose *sawahs* bordered this river because they belonged to the same *subak* that he belonged to. He went on to describe the *subak:* "Group votes are taken by members to determine responsibility for cleaning irrigation canals, planting, regulation of waters, and other issues affecting the crops. The *subak* network rushes decisions concerning any major changes in policy to us with the speed of the waters. Not one bit of news evades even the smallest farmer!"

On the other side of the small shrine, Ketut pointed to a banyan tree at the edge of Mas. The tree trunk, fifteen feet wide at the base, had increased in size as tendrils from the lower branches had taken root. "That's where the cricket match will take place," Ketut said. "It's far enough from the main road so that the fight won't be broken up." He crossed the last small irrigation stream, again making sure to rinse excess dirt off his feet, and sauntered over to the group of thirty-five or forty men who had gathered under the huge tree.

Rice fields

Rice harvest

The arena was not marked with any particular feeling of agitation or excitability. In contrast to the noisy cockfight, where emotions are stirred up and the betting is hot, the overall mood at the cricket match was one of gentlemanly sport. An informal and jolly group of men made quiet wagers with smooth deliberation. Rows of cricket cages lined one edge of the arena. Some of them were covered with emblazoned metal shields recycled from the industrial world—remains of a Coca-Cola can or a Caltex oil container.

Several men erected a small U-shaped bamboo pedestal to support the contenders' cages. Ketut picked up one of his cages and butted it against the other cage on the pedestal. The crickets were now only separated by a sliding partition. Ketut and his opponent now sat in their places, facing each other across a distance of only one foot. Some of the men sported tickle sticks in their hair; others twirled ticklers gently between their fingers as if savoring the sensation of subtle movement. Ketut and his opponent delicately agitated their crickets with the tickle sticks until the creatures were sufficiently stimulated. A referee removed the sliding partition, and the timekeeper signaled the beginning of the match by dropping a punctured coconut shell into a bucket of water. The opponents continued coaxing and irritating with the ticklers until the crickets entered into combat. This intimate and contained battle arrested the attention of every man in the arena, and the small crowd leaned over *en masse* to watch the vicious fighting. Men standing around the mat peered intently over those seated in front of them. Every eye focused on the flurry of wings, on the reaches and grabs of the pincers, on the savage attacks to the

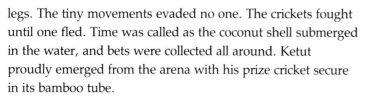
Cricket fights

legs. The tiny movements evaded no one. The crickets fought until one fled. Time was called as the coconut shell submerged in the water, and bets were collected all around. Ketut proudly emerged from the arena with his prize cricket secure in its bamboo tube.

The matches varied in intensity, with many crickets participating in more than one fight. Some of the toughest creatures made return bouts, revealing yet other degrees of strength—the bending of the hind legs when attacked, the tenacious pull of the front legs while pursuing an obvious loser. Jovial gambling continued, cordial but with the emphasis on victory.

Several small portable *warungs* sold coffee, cigarettes, and cookies. Children occasionally ran around the edge of the arena, but for the most part, the men participating in the event seldom changed position for several hours. Late in the afternoon, Ketut withdrew from the contest with a small gain in prize money. He was concerned that his crickets were in need of grooming. "I don't want to be embarrassed by a shabby contender in my stable. I will clean their wings tonight and be sure to coat them with holy water for extra luster."

We returned to Peliatan by a more direct route. Work in the fields had almost stopped. The first tinges of evening chill added an eerie dimension to the end of the daily work.

"We can't linger any more, or we'll have to run from the *leyaks*," Ketut warned. He increased the pace of his step without allowing fear to propel him into a fall.

Children were playing in the palace courtyard. A butterfly flew by, larger than my hand with fingers outstretched. They chased after it until one of them caught it, unsuspecting, and very gently lifted it up by the wings and brought it back to the porch. A young girl made a harness out of thread, and then, with great concentration and care, slipping the harness over the body of the captured butterfly. She wrapped a strand of thread around each wing and fastened another harness over the tail; then she let out the thread five or six feet and allowed it to go slack. The butterfly took off and flew in circles over the children's heads. They laughed and squealed with delight, but, at the same time, they were very careful not to pull on the thread. They played in this way until the creature appeared to tire and did not fly anymore. The girl carefully removed the harness from the butterfly, lifted it onto a hibiscus flower, and went back to play a game with the others. The butterfly tried its wings several times, slowly, hesitantly, then flew up over the thatched roof and out of the courtyard.

By the side of the road, five or six villagers had already settled at a *warung* that had a good reputation. This *warung* drew a regular crowd for *naci champur*, a mixed combination of rice, vegetables, chicken, pork sausages, fried egg, and hot spices. Ketut placed the wrapped cricket cages next to him on a bench and ordered the specialty of the house. He ate his meal in typical Balinese manner: hastily, without conversation, but delicately, scooping the rice with only his right hand. After he had finished, he asked for a glass of hot water, and excused himself to rinse off his hand. He then spent an inordinate amount of time, almost twice as much as he had taken to eat, picking out the remnants of the meal from his teeth. This was an embarrassing form of grooming, especially difficult to conceal in such a public place; but he discreetly cupped his left hand over the bottom part of his face, turned at an oblique angle, and picked his teeth vigorously.

The *warung* owner brought some *kopi* and the atmosphere changed from one of abrupt feeding to lively conversation. Several of Ketut's friends joined him and inquired about his success at the cricket matches. They laughed and joked, occasionally pausing to sip *kopi* and take puffs from their crackling *kreteks*. The banter continued. The cigarettes diminished in size. Kerosene lamps hung all around the *warung*, lending a cabaret atmosphere to the simple food stand. Another man from the *banjar* approached Ketut. He was obviously not in the same mood as the others, and with unseemly haste, several of the men who had occupied the bench cleared away.

"Good evening," the man said to Ketut. "I must speak with you." His voice was low and urgent.

"This is hardly a good time or place. Come to my house when we finish our *kopi*. There we'll be able to talk in private."

The woman who owned the *warung* disappeared into the back. Some people sitting at a table nearby asked the owner's husband what was going on, and he told them in a whisper, "Oh, you know, the usual thing . . . cremation. Ceremonies are so expensive that everybody wants to borrow money. Either that or, even worse, to mortgage their fields. In any

case, it's better that we in the village help him out. Because if we don't, he's bound to sell the land to some rich Javanese."

The whispering disturbed Ketut, who promptly paid for the meal and suggested that we have coffee and cigarettes in his family compound. In the dark, the lane that led from the back of the *warung* to the other side of the *banjar* was almost invisible, and the walk became a challenge for me as I carefully placed each step. We turned in to the small path that led to the compound and found Ibu stoking the lanterns. Ketut greeted her and made brief mention of the neighbor whose visit was imminent. She went into the kitchen to prepare *kopi*. Ketut adjusted the height of the hanging lantern and sat down to unwrap the white cloth that had shielded the crickets.

Ketut's young nephews were studiously inking figures from the Mahabharata that he had drawn for them in pencil. He interrupted them to ask their help in grooming the crickets—a special privilege. They were very excited and scurried off to get the grooming kit. Madé got a small dish of warm water and the other boy, Nyoman, got a vial of scented oil from Ketut's closet. Ketut then added a precise amount of rarefied scent to the water as the boys watched.

"This will make the wings polished and smooth," he said. "Ultra-*halus*."

Ketut opened the first cage in his stable, letting the creature run into his left hand; then he held the body calmly and firmly. He slipped his long thumbnail between the wings and the body, turning the cricket upside down to submerge the wings in the special lubricant. He held its body just above the liquid until the wings were sufficiently coated but not sopping wet.

Meanwhile, the boys hung a small cork ball from the bottom of the lantern. With cock's feathers, they suspended ten string harnesses from the cork; each harness awaited a newly groomed cricket. The delicate apparatus served as a most efficient drying mechanism and was attended by the young assistants. Ketut slipped the first cricket into its harness, its body limp yet mobile, and adjusted the tension. The cricket made its body rigid and buzzed its wings in an outbreak of activity

Time seemed dissolved into minute particles of waiting until the wings were completely dried. Across the courtyard, Ibu had assembled a tall stack of woven palm-leaf containers. Each measuring three inches square, they would be filled with rice sculptures that she had dyed a bright pink, packed into woven molds, and boiled in water to assume new life as vibrant, radiantly colored offerings required for the cremation. Ibu inserted the containers into a large basket, and took up the task of plaiting and cutting more palm leaves into spectacularly shaped offerings. Then she, too, rested from her activity to enjoy a *kretek,* and appeared to fade off into the shadows of the porch.

Just as Ketut placed the last of his prize crickets in its cage, the neighbor entered the courtyard. Ketut motioned for the man to join him and sent one of the boys to bring the *kopi.* He cleared the mat where he was working, and began to prepare the mixture of rice and special additives for the creatures' evening meal. He continued to do this while chatting with the neighbor. They discussed the contents of the mixture and the amount of money that Ketut had won; they talked about mutual friends from the *subak* who had been present at the match, and they shared childhood memories of walks to neighboring village celebrations.

Ketut removed the last cricket from its harness and instructed Nyoman in preparing the food. He watched as the young boy coated the grains of rice and carefully deposited them through the slats of the cages. Madé had returned to the porch carrying a tray with two glasses of *kopi* and now helped his cousin.

The boys fed each cricket until all the rice grains were gone; then they covered the stable with the white cloth and took the creatures to the darkest corner of Ketut's studio. The crickets chirped for some time, but by the time the boys themselves had gone to bed, all was silent except for the talk between Ketut and his neighbor. They retired to the more formal *balé* and continued their conversation in muted voices well into the night.

Woman making offerings

that lasted for several seconds. Then it became still and swayed and turned slightly, its wings glistening under the glow of the warm light. As several more of the crickets emerged from the bath, the ball became a merry-go-round of the most unusual sort.

Flower offerings

ACTIVATED TIME

In the life cycle of the Balinese, there is no ritual of higher spiritual significance than the liberation of a soul through cremation. Usually the joyous celebration is performed just after death. But in many instances a cremation will not occur because of high costs, and the body will be temporarily interred until the family is able to bear the expense. This period of time may be brief, or it may be so lengthy that only the bones remain to be cremated. Cremation is considered to be the ultimate offering, and no obstacle is insurmountable if the desire to elevate the soul is present. The amount of money spent demonstrates respect for the gods and ancestors (and also serves a communal function by keeping personal wealth in check). Anybody who can mortgage paddies, borrow money, sell valuable possessions (such as a cow), or cash in a savings account of stored rice is potentially able to secure a higher place in the heavens for a revered ancestor.

During the weeks following my arrival, Peliatan was very *ramai* indeed. Devotion and fervor increased as the impending cremation signaled a crescendo in celebration that would culminate with the Eka Dasa Rudra, still eight months away. Thousands of bones, sometimes representing many genera-

tions of dead, had been dug up and splendidly enshrined on platforms amidst a shower of offerings. Magnificently displayed, the bones awaited the blessings of priests whose presence was demanded by every family participating in the cremations. Because the schedules of the priests were so jammed, they roamed the village all day long, supervising the construction of towers and offerings. They recited Hindu and Buddhist incantations and prayers necessary to purify and free the soul from its earthly bonds. For all these services, the priests were paid handsomely.

Weeks flew by full of an overwhelming amount of ritual work. Empty time—everyday tasks, casual socializing, and the relaxed atmosphere surrounding cricket grooming—was temporarily suspended. Time was now activated by the gods, who had descended from their dwellings in the heights of the Gunung Agung to occupy shrines all over the island. In the royal courts of Peliatan, crews worked until dawn, assembling boat-size vessels that were then filled with offerings. Herds of bull sarcophagi were artfully constructed in the outer courtyard of the palace. In a huge open field next to the Temple of Death, low-caste families erected a communal pyre. They

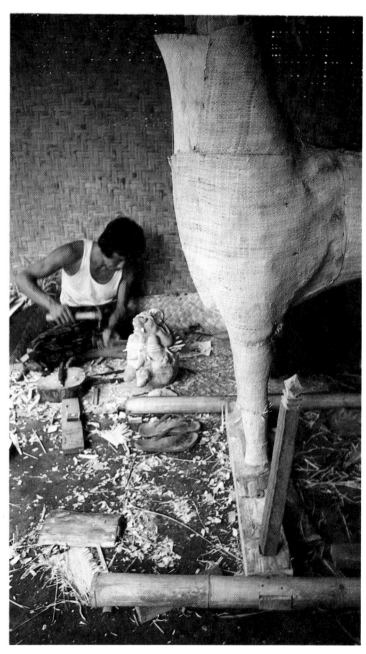

Construction of ritual objects for the cremation ceremony

constructed their offerings under the roofs of two long pavilions. Each family cubicle, separated from the next by a thin bamboo partition, overflowed with palm-leaf sculptures, rice cookies, and cakes. In the center of each cubicle, stacks of cloth surrounded the bones of the ancestors resting on elevated platforms. Brilliant silks, red Chinese brocades, traditional Javanese bone and *kris* batiks, sacred weavings patterned with ancient religious symbols and motifs—all ensured that the cremation pyre would be ablaze in the radiance of beneficent and righteous spirits. In Ketut's compound, everyone who was in any way related took part in the feverish preparations. Ketut himself seldom slept for more than a few hours each night. He had forgotten his obsession with the crickets and was rarely seen beyond the porch where the *singha* sarcophagus grew more sumptuous with the passing of each day.

Carrying offerings to the temple

Ibu, in the midst of all her work, had managed to tell me briefly of an annual ritual about to take place in Tenganan. This Bali Aga village, in the remote eastern part of the island, was renowned for its *kain gringsing.* These "flaming cloths," recognized by the Balinese as documents of spiritual origin, were used by the people of Tenganan in rituals of ancestor worship. "Tonight the mating rituals will take place," Ibu said. "And tomorrow, there's the *Prang Duri.* Men, and even small boys, fight matches resolved when the first blood is drawn. But it's really only a small scratch, and it's all in good fun. Besides, you won't be the only tourist there," she assured me. "Everyone wants to see the holy cloths that the villagers will be wearing for the festivities."

The next morning, I left the family compound just before dawn. Ketut had completed the brilliant wings for the *singha* and was crawling off to sleep as I started up my small Honda motorbike. Dawn on the paddies was not filled with the usual activity, since most of the rice had been harvested and many of the neighboring villages were also busy with preparations for their own mass cremations. Several kilometers to the east, a solitary farmer with his sacred cow plowed a flooded paddy. The road wound past many small villages, through the bustling center of Klungkung, a large market town, down a mammoth river valley and across the expanse of a modern narrow bridge, up a steep fern-covered hill, and finally reached a plateau on the eastern coast of the island. The Gunung Agung

Temple gate, Tenganan

loomed in front of me. The road continued along the coast for thirty kilometers, past fields that were flat and level. Burned *sawahs* awaited irrigation water in this more arid part of the island. As I made a sharp turn, the Gunung Agung disappeared behind rolling foothills; the road ended at the entrance to the walled village of Tenganan.

The village was small, isolated, and self-contained. A flight of narrow stairs ascending the tower at the corner of the eastern and southern walls was the only entrance. Interior and exterior stairs converged at the top of the tower. Several people could stand on the tiny waiting pavilion there, but the stairways were only wide enough for one person at a time. The entire village was visible from the tower. All communal *balés* stood in one long row—the central axis of the village. From beneath these structures, the gentle sounds of a creek could be heard, lending a pastoral tone to the village. But on this day, because of the *Prang Duri,* festive villagers, tourists from other parts of the island, and foreigners, converging on the elevated fighting arena, added tension to the atmosphere. Eerie clangs and tinkling, from an ancient iron-keyed metallophone, rippled throughout the village.

Kain gringsing

Rejang

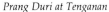
Prang Duri at Tenganan

The village was alive with activity: directly in front of the largest community *balé*, thirty men and as many young boys huddled in groups of fighters, supporters, referees, and would-be contenders. Piles of discarded thorny palm branches—the bloody weapons—littered the ground. Several men never left the platform, and waited eagerly behind their rattan shields for another bout. Young boys paraded in droves, valiantly displaying their bloody scratches. All the while, deep, mellow-toned gongs accompanied the laughter of attacking warriors and the creaking of three hand-turned ferris wheels. Only the girls and women watching the "wars," trancelike and silent behind staked fences, sheltered by the eaves of the community *balé*, provided a glimpse of the solemnity of the event.

The "wars" continued until early afternoon. Communal meals, served on huge platters, complemented the festivities and the crowd's excitement. Warriors sat in circles in front of their family compounds, and other villagers busied them-

selves with preparations for the temple ceremonies. An evening performance of the Arja by a traveling troupe, the Rejang, and all-night offering rituals were still to come. The ferris wheels, which children piled onto, creaked and spun into the evening. A *gamelan* at the temple announced the start of the Rejang, a dance ritual known for its timeless quality and meditative length. Just after the beginning of the Rejang, I decided to depart for Peliatan, as darkness would soon obscure the unfamiliar road.

I had already been warned about demons and evil spirits lurking at the crossroads, especially at dusk, and I became extra sensitive to the emptiness of the road. Small winged bugs formed a dense wall in front of me, obstructing my vision and making steering difficult. I imagined the ancestors of Tenganan laughing at my speedy getaway. But after I had gone many tense kilometers, the bugs dispersed as the terrain changed from flat and arid to terraced, moist, and humid again. As I left the coast, the moistness increased, and just

A priest blesses the cremation offerings

before dark, erratic patterns of pointed-winged black bats festooned the sky. Occasionally, they dived in front of the motorbike lamp. Their shrill whine penetrated the air. The sky became pocked with the bats, which in a frenzied flight into the night had fled their homes in a nearby cave. The road continued past two more caves, and then dim lights from Klungkung marked my return to a more humanly populated part of the island. The crispness of the night winds revealed an endless universe of dazzling stars that illuminated the road through the paddies until I arrived in Peliatan.

On the night before the mass cremations, Ibu's family gathered in the compound to perform the rituals that would enable her father's soul to embark on its journey to heaven. A *dalang* and four musicians filled the house with music and tales, entertaining the ancestors and gods who now occupied the family's shrines. Incense was burned. A *pedanda*, seated on an elevated platform, recited incantations of purification and blessing. He rang a prayer bell, occasionally punctuating his gestures by flicking holy water and flowers onto the family below. In the center of the courtyard, at the base of the high priest's platform, four men, symbolizing the cardinal points, sat on a bench and read the family history from *lontar* texts. Their voices rose above the soft prayers of the priest and the musicians' melodies, creating a mass of ritual penetrating the senses with sweetness of sound, incense, and mysterious emotions.

The family crowded around a huge boatlike vessel that overflowed with offerings. Arrays of tiny baskets containing dried flowers and symbolic palm-leaf sculptures, which the women had prepared over the course of a month, were to become the sacred fuel of the cremation fire. The eldest son picked up a miniature *prau* and began to tell of the soul's very long journey. He called out in an animated yet entranced voice:

Flame burning at the bow
Illuminate my path
Over boundless oceans
Gliding on smooth peaceful waters
Constantly ascending to the flaming heavens.

Beginning of the cremation procession

As he spoke, it seemed that he'd become the captain of the ship, assuming the voice of his ancestor. "Gather around me, my children, so I see you as I depart on this blissful voyage." Rocking the miniature boat in front of his face, he formed a spyglass by cupping one eye with his free hand. He surveyed the familiar faces: brothers, children, grandchildren, tiny infants and toddlers, distant relatives, friends.

The family had become one entity surrounding the vessel, circling three times while the telling of the journey was completed.

Before the pyres are ignited, a priest gives advice and
counsel to the soul of the dead:

Thy hair will return to the bushes,
thy skin to earth, thy flesh to the waters, thy blood to fire,
thy sinews to roots, thy bones to wood, thine eyes to Sun and
Moon,
thy head to the sphere, thy breath to the wind.
Thy voice returns to earthquake and thunder,
thy soul returns to Taya;
Do not forget the wise lessons,
keep them in thy mind and do not forget them,
these my last instructions to thee.

Butterfly of the World!
thou fliest with "soul," "other soul," "bad soul," "no soul."
An end has come to thy being "forefather soul";
thou art "Divine Forefather," for I have shipped thee over.
Now bow down and make the sign of worship for me,
for I am the incarnation of the Highest God.
Butterfly of the World,
take the soul of the infant on thy hip and bring it to thy forehead,
to twelve fingers' breadth aloft of it;
the soul will leave, the force of life has been solved.

After the cremation, the family gathered up the remaining
pile of ashes and several bits of bone, put them into a small
vessel, and took them in a carriage procession to the sea. A
priest removed the urn to a boat, rowed out past the breakers
at the shore until he was barely visible, then scattered the contents
out over the vast waters, to the wind and high up into the sky.

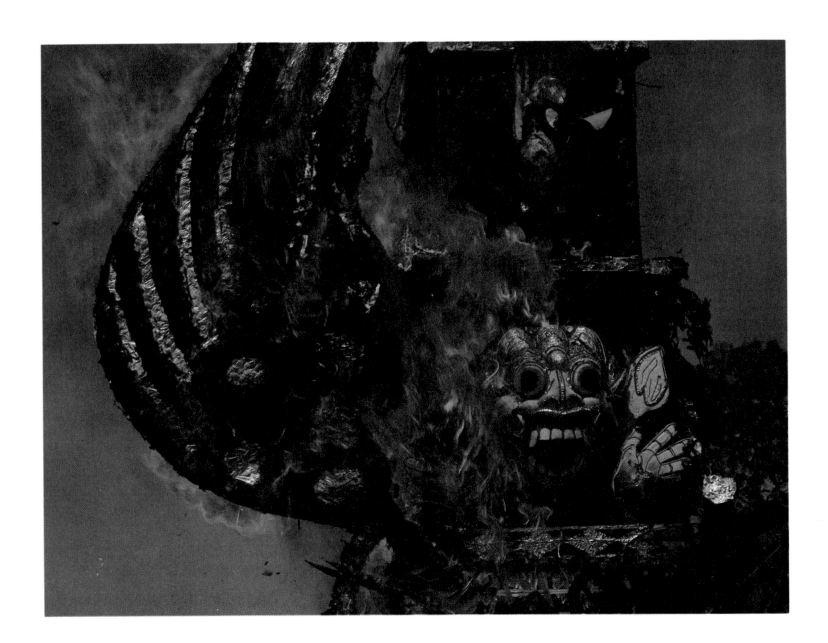

CELEBRATION AT
THE TEMPLE OF DEATH

Dark clouds descended on the central rice plains. A sudden gust of wind blew through the rain, curtain-like in its density. Several motorcyclists insisted on penetrating the thick torrents until the impossibility of the task became evident, then sought the most immediate shelter, the *balé banjar*. Roaring rain competed with improvised, flirtatious melodies coming from the back of the *balé*, where a group of children shared the keys of an oversized *gangsa*. The children quickened their beat in accompaniment to the swift, harsh gale pounding the palm fronds all around the central pavilion. Their playing seemed to temper the downpour; the wind faded momentarily. Some of them began to play on the stage area and spontaneously choreographed a monkey dance. They hopped around to the rhythm and roamed among the villagers, totally absorbed in their monkey identities, then became young musicians again for another turn at the huge instrument.

On a small adjacent *balé*, a group of men sat with their fighting cocks. The fierce winds roused their irrepressible birds. Petty matches and bets were arranged in the background, but did not attract much attention. Other villagers walked into the covered *balé banjar* and sat down for a coffee break, laying down the banana leaves they had used for protection against the rain. A priest dressed all in white walked along the road sheltered by a black umbrella—his composure was unruffled by the torrent. Farmers with bundles of vegetables suspended on bamboo rods trotted home from the fields with great ease; the downpour seemed irrelevant.

Tinkling in the distance, a portable *gamelan* approached the community center, first challenging, then gently overpowering the children's playful music. In uninterrupted cadence, a procession of women carrying tiered offerings on their heads lifted the corners of their sarongs as they passed through shallow puddles in front of the *balé banjar*. Behind them, the *gamelan* played out simple ceremonial melodies. Three huge gongs, roped onto a large pole, reverberated along the path of the procession. Drummers, their instruments slung over their shoulders, escorted the Barong Landung, a pair of towering masked puppets.

The Barongs' masks, and the wood from which they were made, pass through ceremonies of purification, animation and connection, and transformation. The first ceremony, purification, removes indelible stains or bad spirits acquired by the wood during its attachment to the earth. Purification is achieved through offerings of gold, silver, and copper—each one in exact proportions—which are magically combined to become one entity. After this ceremony, the wood becomes receptive to the Spirit of the Mask.

Even when the mask is carved and painted, the Barong, a great Protecting Spirit whose mask must be attached to its body, is still considered "dead," just as if it were a felled tree, inhabited only by a ghost. In the ceremony of animation and connection, a high priest sanctifies the mask and brings it back to life, with spiritual properties.

But the purification and the animation and connection ceremonies do not yet involve the actual wearing of the mask by a devoted performer. With the third ceremony of transformation, the strength of omnipotence enters into the mask. It becomes infused with an active Spirit capable of protection and the execution of magic. This transformation occurs at either of two sites: a large temple or Holy Place, or the graveyard.

The Barongs, whose bodies were hoisted on the shoulders of two especially strong actors, were each fifteen feet tall. Dancing and sashaying, the ghastly black-masked-male-with-buckteeth appeared quite harmless. In fact, his manner was extraordinarily sensual as he occasionally bumped against his partner, the female Barong. Her white mask and serene expression indicated a nobility and refinement that was utterly contrary to her provocative behavior.

The jovial couple were journeying to the forest of their origin where they were to be enshrined as Protecting Spirits during the anniversary celebrations at the Pura Dalem in the Sacred Monkey Forest of a neighboring village. The gods, attracted by the Barongs' presence, would descend to inhabit the temple, further heightening the atmosphere of thanksgiving. Nightly entertainment would be splendid, and the gods, pleased by this added demonstration of faith, would bestow blessings of grace, goodness, and wealth to the villagers.

All along the main road of the village and out of Peliatan the Barongs told bawdy jokes. They struck seductive postures and then danced together in capricious movements. They entered a small lane that led through the paddies and finally arrived at the Pura Dalem in the center of the forest.

During this ceremony, performed in the middle of the night, the garments and mask are put on a stand near the offerings, opposite the candidate. If the ceremony takes place at the graveyard, the base of the candidate's seat must be made of three human skulls. If the ceremony is performed at a Holy Place, the base of the seat is made of young yellow coconuts. Then, in the successful ceremony, the mask receives a visitation from one of the beneficent gods. When contact is truly established, the candidate promptly lifts the mask to his face and enters into a state of trance. He runs around the area of the ceremony and dances spontaneously. He gazes on the altar where the offerings are made. In this receptive state the Consciousness of the Divine will guide his every sway until sacred powers have been infused into the mask. The ceremony ends when the candidate, leaving the state of trance, collapses. The priest catches him and sprinkles him with holy water. If the Spirit has not entered into the mask, the ceremony will be repeated at another auspicious time.

There was a rumor moving through the village that Kakul was going to dance in the Topéng at the celebration of the Pura Dalem. Since I was not familiar with this particular dancer, the rumor had no special significance for me, but I sensed an air of excitement, of eagerness, as the festivities rolled on.

I asked several people in Peliatan about this man Kakul, and heard varied and conflicting stories.

"Oh, he's just an old has-been dancer," said one very cosmopolitan and well-traveled musician. "He dances the traditional old style, which we all find very boring now."

"Kakullll!" giggled a beautiful young dancer. She turned toward her girl friends and they all giggled, too.

"Yes, I remember him," said Anom, a dancer from the royal family in Peliatan. Anom had been on a world tour with Kakul and other Balinese dancers and musicians in 1952. She had been twelve years old at the time, but her memories were still fresh and alive. "Kakul danced in the passageways of the railway cars in America. Most of us slept as soon as we found a seat, but Kakul serenaded us in a voice so tender that we felt

Barong Landung

as if we were once again at home. He sang Arja ballads to soothe his yearnings for his beloved new second wife. Oh, he missed her so much that my girl friends and I were sad, too. But he also played many pranks on us. Sometimes he fooled us by sleeping in his hotel room until just before performance time; then he insisted that there was plenty of time left. As proof he pointed to his wristwatch, which obviously meant nothing. What a rascal! In England, of course, he wore a proper black British bowler. Kakul laughed around the world."

"Kakul," reminisced Anak Agung Gedé Mandera, the noble Prince who led Peliatan's famous *gamelan* and dancers. "Yes, he is a most respected dancer." The Prince spoke graciously, in a voice suited to courtly Balinese life. "Kakul perpetuates the dance styles refined by the late Raja of Sukawati, Anak Agung Gedé Raka, now Revered Ancestor. During his lifetime, our Revered Ancestor perfected the style of Jauk, which is a great work of interpretative solo choreography, and Kakul has the agility, grace, and nuance needed to dance with the rapid rhythms of the Jauk's drum solo. When the Raja died in 1948, his lavish cremation destroyed the family fortune; no matter, he has surely received a high incarnation." The Prince paused, then imitated Kakul's nimble gestures. "It was a shame that during the world tour in the 1950's there was not enough time to include Kakul's performance of Jauk. But Kakul's most startling performance is as Topéng Tua. He is certainly the most faithful to the true ancient character of this mask. His *taksu* is striking."

"He has lost his *taksu*," said another villager.

"His humor is so ironic there's no one like him!" proclaimed a fan.

"There are better dancers," said someone else.

Competition between Kakul and a younger dancer stirred up a whirling cloud of gossip in the days before the Topéng performance. But the presence of a Javanese witch doctor on the first night of the celebration at the Pura Dalem in the neighboring village provided another topic of gossip. Among all the *warungs* that filled the vicinity just outside the temple

Rangda

area, his array of potions attracted the largest crowd; and everyone had a black magic story to tell.

"Did you hear about the woman who has been invaded by such Forces of the Wind that she is always gasping?"

"*Aduuuh!*"

"It must have been black magic!"

"And what about the dancer who put on the mask without making appropriate offerings, or perhaps his spirit was not pure, or his *taksu* was challenged. After he removed his mask, he went crazy and finally ate the sap from a poisonous tree and killed himself."

"*Béh!*"

Music from the Wayang Kulit already in progress in the outer courtyard of the temple lured the crowd. Behind a translucent screen, the *dalang* sat and manipulated each puppet into postures so lilting and dynamic that the shadows visible to the audience on the other side took on a life of their own. He was the narrator, commentator, and translator. He portrayed mortal beings, immortal beings, and incarnate gods— all the characters of the story. Almost everyone listened attentively to the unfolding drama, but in the front rows youngsters sprawled on the mats that covered the earthen floor dozed on top of each other. During the philosophical discourses between gods and kings, young lovers rendezvoused at the *warungs*. They sought out the quiet areas surrounding the temples or ventured into the fields. The drama climaxed in several unresolved battles that woke sleeping children. Excited by the magical voice of the *dalang*, the mysterious music, and the sounds of puppets hitting against each other behind the screen, the children yelled, cheered the hero, and laughed at the jokes of the attendants. In the hours just before dawn, goodness vanquished evil. The *dalang*, who for six hours had recounted the ancient lore, closed the lid on the box containing the puppets and chanted *mantras* bidding the spirits return to their homes.

On my walk back to Peliatan, the road became brightly illuminated with silver light. Families were still carrying offerings to the temple. Faces passed me in the jungle, clearly revealed in the glow of the waxing moon. When I reached the village edge, a pack of dogs barked after me until I neared Ketut's *banjar*. Loud and vicious, they backed off at the moment before attack, probably fearing that I was the stranger from a village that ate dogmeat. I adopted the curse: "Kill dogs. Eat dogs," and ignored them as best I could.

On the day of the Topéng performance, the whole village was involved with the peripheral activities of ritual. Women arranged offerings in silver bowls to carry to the temple for blessing by the priests. Men adorned themselves with bright waist scarves and ritual headcloths. After the midday procession of offerings, the outer courtyard of the temple was transformed into a cockfight arena. Women and children continued to bring offerings into the inner sanctuary as the cockfighting went on through the day.

Late in the afternoon, vendors set up tables on the roadside opposite the temple area. A brief drizzle threatened to disturb the effortless pace of activity, but the rituals would continue through any downpour that might occur. Arm in arm, young girls paraded in their best clothes, while the boys, also arm in arm, passed by in separate groups. Friendships had been sparked during the performance of the Wayang Kulit the night before. New couples had returned to their respective families, keeping a secret that their friends would soon discover. They all looked beautiful, and greeted one another with warm, knowing laughter. The sun set. Clouds dispersed; the full moon rose and an unusual brilliance filled the evening sky.

The road just outside the Pura Dalem was filled. There was much activity at the portable *warungs*, some of them so elaborately assembled that when they were lined up, one next to another, they appeared to be permanent structures. On the outskirts of this *warung* district, several table vendors of modest means sold all kinds of food and drink: sweet bean cakes and coffee; rice with *gado-gado* and fried eggs; palm wine and *arak*. Boys and girls flirted; the old men teased toddlers who were not yet old enough to participate in the raucous play of older children. Fluid processions of offerings in and out of the sacred areas continued.

The outer courtyard where the Topéng performance was to take place was jammed. A tight circle at the front of the courtyard spilled over to the side areas where musicians were setting up their instruments. Children's voices rang above the chatter, and the crowd swayed and murmured. Long strands of finely fringed palm branches were stretched along the periphery of the courtyard behind the musicians. Every few yards the outer border was broken by altars loaded with flower offerings. Two stone guardians covered with black-and-white-checked cloth protected the main entrance to the inner courtyard. Red hibiscus flowers were tucked behind their ears. Immediately behind the guardians, the towering split gates rose in a splendor of flickering candles, the glow at the apex merging with the fullness of the moon.

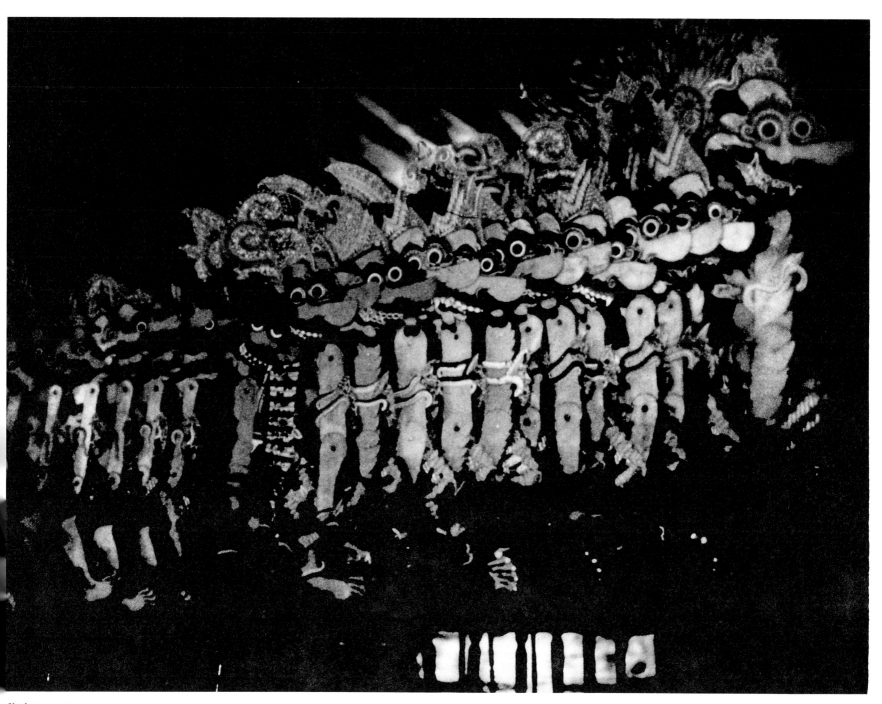

Shadow puppets

Prayer flags

Inside the courtyard, backstage preparations for the entertainment had begun. Attendants wrapped white cloths around the upper torsos of a group of young women dancers. Next, bright yellow and green ceremonial sarongs, painted with gold floral patterns, were wound around, each layer more tightly than the last, until they severely limited the dancers' movements. Children watched in amazement as their friends were transformed into splendorous creatures; the smallest nuance in wrapping provided occasion for giggles and sighs. Then the attendants attached twenty feet of yellow chest binding to the waist of the dancers' sarongs. As the dancers turned slowly at the opposite end, the ribbons wound up their slim torsos until they were encased in the richly ornamented costumes, their bodies held rigid yet supple. One dancer tried bending, swaying, taking several tiny steps to test the boundaries of her movements. Only her shoulders and arms, lower legs and feet were not bound. The flowing train of the sarong emerged from the inner casing, freely spilling out between her feet.

On a dimly lit pavilion in the corner of the courtyard, the five actors of the Topéng troupe were unpacking costumes from a mound of bamboo cases. Although the actors were nearly obscured by the darkness, peals of continuous shrill laughter were audible from their dressing area. A short man, gesturing with considerable style, commanded everyone's attention. The other actors responded to him with a vigor and humor equaling his own. His laughter was startling, unusual, and appeared strange, except that it induced belly-clutching laughter among the troupe, and before long, another crowd of children formed around the actors' *balé*. Children pointed and whispered: "Kakul!"

As soon as the actors finished dressing they became quiet. They moved in a disciplined manner. They adjusted their brightly colored capes, which caught distant lamplight and reflected it in shimmering golden swirls. Beaded collars glistened and tinkled faintly as the actors placed them on their velvet shirts. A girl dancer tied several additional flowers into her hair; a handsome young male dancer made last-minute adjustments in his makeup. Everyone moved very fast. Children ran to the front of the courtyard. The *gamelan* began playing lightly, and the first drumbeats signaled the start of the entertainment. Activity slowed in the troupe's pavilion. The actors unpacked their masks, and Kakul's face was solemn as he removed each mask from its cloth wrapping. He lifted a single flower bud in front of his chest and folded his hands in prayer. The sound of a gong coming through the split gate entrance announced the first dance.

In the packed outer courtyard the overture had begun with the Pendet, a ritual offering dance performed by four young women. The *gamelan* sounded out with continuous deep gong tones and mesmerizing whirring notes as the dancers gently pelted the crowd with corsages. The effect of the music, the dancers, and the shower of fragrant blossoms was nearly overwhelming.

Immediately after the Pendet dancers exited in a snake formation through the split gates, a young girl appeared, poised in hypnotic stillness. She seemed to await direction from the *gamelan*. A gong sounded; the dancer, creating the illusion of a hieroglyph, lifted her arms in unison until her elbows reached shoulder height. The drum beat rapidly, and her wide entranced eyes darted left and right, glittering in the lamplight. The clinking of tiny cymbals released her into a rapid walk down the steps and around the courtyard. Her fingers moved more fervently as the music quickened. She swayed, fluttering her golden wings, arms gracefully beating the air— lifting her up, it seemed, above the flickering candles on the gate. She was joined by two nymphlike dancers, and with rare control—in children still so young—the trio enacted a drama of extraordinary intensity. Their own identities were com-

pletely obliterated; here, heavenly souls recounted ancient myths of the Legong.

During a battle scene of ambiguous results, the Legong dancers withdrew through the stone gates, abruptly terminating their dazzling performance. No one in the audience seemed to mind that the combat had continued offstage without resolution. The overture proceeded uninterrupted.

In the middle of the split gate entrance, a young man, the Warrior, held himself erect in contained ferocity; only the subtle shaking of his shell crown revealed his power. Beating drums, characteristic of the Baris, accelerated; with cocklike speed, the Warrior flicked his head to the right, looked up and down with minute movements, then turned to the left, his eyes darting above, then below, as if assessing the road. Having thus prepared himself for attack from any direction, he raised his left hand to his brow and contemplated his next move in repose, with great concentration. A drum challenged his composure. He swayed, rising onto his toes but, with extreme control, contained his energy once again and focused on the march ahead.

Triumphantly displaying his regal mane, he descended the steps, solidly planting each foot as if conquering the incline of an enemy territory. Every shimmering glass bead on his costume magnified his aura of grandeur. He defiantly paraded in front of the *gamelan*. His eyes darted with the sounds of a large gong. Bronze keys clanked, first in curious modulation, then in rhythmic agitation, signaling an imminent attack. The shell crown shook as the Warrior prepared for this encounter; tinges of sadness revealed a more somber aspect of his character. The drummer beat a slow lament, then increased the speed. Flinging himself into an aggressive stance, the Warrior rotated his neck with the fervor of a tiger. Then he released himself, spinning round on one foot. Layers of brilliant cloth strips, hanging in swirls from his chest, flew around him. The *gamelan* immediately changed tempo, culminating in booming gongs of victory. Now posed with his balance firmly maintained on one leg, the Warrior accentuated his meditation: all forces within him resolved, he bowed reverently; then withdrew behind the gates. The sparkling costumes, glittering collars studded with colored beads and reflecting mirror chips, wide-glaring eyes darting from side to side, elevating wings, golden crowns, flamelike headpieces—all had radiated the heat of inner fire, a vibrance and intensity that I had never before experienced.

The lull in performance was immediately filled by excited chatter. Children imitating the sound of the *gamelan* squirmed against each other in eager anticipation. Several people left in a hurry to get coffee or sweets and returned to find their places taken by bold youngsters. People turned and talked to one another, their arms flying and circling in mimicry or criticism of the performance.

A tinkling of bronze keys was barely audible, but in an instant the entire *gamelan* sprang to life, interlaced with the sounds of flutes and gongs. Conversation stopped. In the gateway, a dancer of regal bearing appeared; palms outward, his quivering hands concealed his masked face. The *gamelan* changed pace, and the dancer's hands came to a firm stop directly in front of his mask. Slowly, he parted his arms in one continuous sweep, revealing a character of strength and refinement: the eyes of the mask bulging and round, teeth gleaming white. His elaborate headdress indicated his high rank, that of a Prime Minister. Everyone in the audience recognized this traditional character, performed as a prelude to the Topéng drama proper.

The actor gyrated his shoulders in tiny backward circles, drawing himself up to monumental stature; then, exhaling, he dropped his chest, and with a piercing gaze checked the path in front of him. It seemed that the more imperceptible the movement of the actor, the more real the mask became. Now confident of a worthy reception, the Prime Minister descended the staircase boldly. He danced in silence, reveling in the elegance of his costume. He pondered his responsibilities as Prime Minister and made a dignified exit as soon as he had completed the brief pantomime.

A second masked Prime Minister appeared. He also wore an ornate headdress, but his teeth, bared in a fierce snarl, revealed a manner that was much cruder than that of the refined Prime Minister who preceded him. His hair was wild and rumpled yet somehow majestic. His belligerent attitude was tempered by an improvisation that deviated slightly from the traditional choreography but brought recognition and laughter from the audience nonetheless. He exited rather abruptly, and when the third character, the Topéng Tua, entered, the enthusiastic crowd stirred. The *gamelan* played his theme.

Motionless at the top of the steps, the weary Old Man stood hunched over, breathing heavily, until he had mustered enough strength to bring his hands together in a *mudra*. He remained in meditation for an instant, his wise eyes concentrating on the imaginary blossom over his heart. A poignant solo flute beckoned him, and when he raised his head, he appeared dazed. The audience was amused by his bewilderment, but the Old Man ignored them and proceeded down the stone steps in a style befitting a Revered Elder. The restraint and precision of his dance emphasized the venerable expression of his mask. But at the bottom of the steps he faltered, and careened toward a group of children. They reeled back, uncertain if he would really fall, and just at the last moment, the Old Man regained his balance. The children ridiculed his weakness and lack of control. The Old Man straightened himself, then he danced, slowly and gracefully, all around the stage. His movements were exactly those of a frail King, and I wondered if the actor was truly an old man.

At the base of the steps he paused, scratching his head as if remembering a past glory. He tentatively began a spry imitation of a youthful ruler, but lost his balance again and whirled off toward the orchestra, almost falling on top of the drummer.

He panted, hesitated on tiptoe, then frantically lifted his cape and began scratching his chest. The children rollicked out of control. Suddenly, the Old Man began scratching his body all over, responding to each new itch so slowly that it was a wonder he ever soothed his discomfort. He finally reached up with both hands into his shaggy scalp and scratched diligently in one area until he caught the culprit, delicately pulled it out, and held it in front of his eyes. The flute interjected a tender

The Old Man

The Penesar

The Dalem

melody. The Old Man's wooden eyes appeared to swell with tears of joy. Then he waddled over to a crowd of children and triumphantly showed them the louse. He pressed it between his two thumbnails until it was "dead," and flicked it into the dirt. The children shared his delight and the Old Man turned and danced off as gleefully as he could manage, only to be interrupted by another tiny bothersome creature. The crowd loved his antics; the adults recognized in his dilemma an experience common to all people. The Old Man reluctantly climbed the steps and exited, leaving the crowd in good spirits for the beginning of the Topéng drama.

The music ceased. Modulated, booming, and pompous, the Penesar's voice served to herald the impending performance. Even though he was still in the inner courtyard and could not be seen, his operatic proclamation resounded throughout the temple area. When he finished his aria, he bolted through the split gates, down the steps, and into the

outer courtyard, striding past the *gamelan* and stopping only when he reached the edge of the audience.

"Aha ha ha ha. Heeee heeee hee. *Béh!* What's this?"

In good humor, the Penesar chanted to the crowd in Kawi, translating into common Balinese for the benefit of most of the villagers. He astutely recited the genealogy of the district's ancient dynasties, occasionally shouting as he recounted a particularly dramatic period of history. He culminated his soliloquy by referring to the celebration in progress and elaborating on the religious significance of the temple's anniversary. He strutted in circles, speaking with authority, but his flamboyant gestures and his mask, which covered only the upper part of his face and nose, suggested the taint of a braggart. The Penesar stopped in mid-sentence.

"Tuut, Tuut, Tuut, Tuut, Tuut, Tuut, Tuut, Tuut!" he called in machine-gun rhythm. "That guy's such a worm. He's so irresponsible. Why can't he be diligent like all the rest of us? He's always late and I'm stuck waiting all alone for our King, a ruler of true refinement. I always have to take care of everything by myself."

The *gamelan* began to play softly, and the Penesar danced in amusement.

"Aha! Ha ha ha! Wait a minute." He signaled the *gamelan* to stop. "Where is that guy?" The Penesar continued dancing; the *gamelan* picked up his lead.

Meanwhile the Kartala, affectionately called "Tuut" (short for Ketut), entered unnoticed except by the audience. They tittered as the sly, lackadaisical attendant shadowed the Penesar, mimicking his dance. Unaware of these antics, the Penesar was upset by the crowd's change in mood. He stopped his dance and backed into the skinny Kartala, whose half-mask expressed a slack and dim-witted nature.

"*Aduh!*" gasped the Penesar, as he turned and confronted the Kartala. "You idiot! You scared me half to death. Haven't I got enough problems without you hanging around in the shadows like some kind of *leyak!* Look at you, dressed like a slob—what will our King think of *me?*"

In his exasperation the Penesar had grabbed the Kartala, suspending him by the back of his beaded collar. The Penesar released him, but only after the Kartala folded into a posture of resignation.

"Dear Older Brother," the Kartala pleaded in mock shame. "Surely I cannot be expected to present a countenance as refined and composed as yours. You who are so close to our King. You who know all the etiquette and manners of the court." He bowed sarcastically several times to beg forgiveness for his irreverent behavior.

The Penesar continued berating him: "Tell me, how is it that you arrive just after I've finished my work? Never mind. It's obvious that you just want to eat. You only care about the ceremonies when the offerings are ready for you to eat, that's

it. Then you'll probably hide in a corner of the temple and sleep. You're lazy. You're selfish. How do you ever expect to come close to the King? Your attitude stinks!"

The members of the *gamelan* stopped playing and joined in the audience's laughter.

"Dear Older Brother, you're right. Of course I'm far from the inner court; working in the garden, I don't cultivate the dirt under my fingernails as you do."

The insults became more outrageous. Always conscious of the base use of the left hand and the public use of the right, the audience exploded when the Kartala offered his left hand to the Penesar as a token of apology. They cheered the two actors until finally the jokes led to accusations about the Kartala's lack of control of his bodily functions, and he countered by accusing the Penesar of farting in the royal court.

"This is inexcusable! Your attitude is deplorable, your thoughts are in the pigsty! You will doubtless pay for your reckless speech by reincarnating as a dog!"

There ensued a jovial chase around the courtyard, which the Penesar concluded by calling out in exasperation: "TTTT-UUUU-UTTT!"

The Kartala relented and asked, "Well, what's your problem, anyway? You got troubles with the Officials? You planning to emigrate to Sumatra?"

The Penesar endured this attitude. "I will tolerate your manner, since you are essentially stupid, but you must listen carefully now, because affairs of state are in jeopardy. We must come together for this celebration and bid our King to honor us with His presence."

The *gamelan* played the introductory music for the Dalem's entrance. The Kartala obediently sat on the ground next to the *gamelan,* while the Penesar knelt on one knee and concentrated on the imminent arrival. In this posture, as taut as a tiger, he brought his hands together to form a refined gesture used to address the high caste. He turned his head toward the gate entrance, asking for forgiveness before speaking to a celestial being. He began a yearning and glorious song. The Kartala translated the canticle into common Balinese:

The air is transformed. It is all gentleness and prettiness.

The *gamelan* played a soft crescendo, then decreased, resolving the tender jangle of bronze keys in a majestic solo. The drum joined in syncopated rhythm, causing a change in melody, and the *gamelan* became serene. The Penesar continued his yearning song until the Dalem, in all his regal splendor, appeared seated on the rim of a chair at the top of the steps, his feet far from the ground.

The Dalem began his dance while still seated. Slowly reaching for the Jewel of his crown, he hesitated for a brief instant, the tips of his right fingers resting in contact with the Jewel. He tilted his head in homage to the All-Encompassing Reality, then, with a flick of the wrist, he extended his hand and addressed his Attendants.

The Penesar sang:

See how Fine and Elegant are the Clothes of our King
He is Graced with Knowledge and Charm
His every motion causing a Shimmer of Awe.

The Dalem performed a series of *mudras*. Gathering the currents around his throne, he brought his wrists together, touching them in front of his heart. He dispersed the air, extending his open palms to the crowd, then formed a *mudra* with each hand just to the side of his breast. The forward thrust of his chest, accentuated by the wafting sound of the flutes, appeared to raise him in flight. The *mudras* completed, he began to descend from his throne with ease and finesse.

Placing his steps as if on clouds, he gestured to the Penesar and Kartala. The Penesar served as the Dalem's "voice." The Kartala translated the ancient language into conversational Balinese. The audience, transfixed by a Presence of such magnificence, silently attended to each utterance. They followed the Dalem's every movement.

The Dalem danced around the arena. He changed direction as if propelled by the tranquil rush of the flute melody to which he had relinquished his will. He became the current of breath.

In the background, the Kartala tried to imitate the Dalem's majestic gestures, but to no avail. Finally, the Kartala bowed reverently and made way as the Dalem began his ascent back to the throne. Instructions regarding the mandatory rituals had been completed. The Dalem's walk was deliberate yet sublime, the tempo set by his breath in meditation as he rose to the top of the steps.

Just as the long train of the Dalem's costume disappeared behind the gates, without any transition at all, the repeating staccato drum led the musicians into a new, frenzied rhythm. Three masked actors descended through the gates so swiftly that their entry seemed almost supernatural. They wore ridiculous and grotesque masks. They waved their arms around their heads. Dancing frantically through the arena, they passed so fast that sparks flew as their beaded collars brushed against each other.

From amid this blur of motion, the first masked character emerged, truly ludicrous. His beaded collar was reminiscent of the one worn by the Dalem, but it was impossible to believe that this could be the same actor. He tried to speak, flapping his movable jaws without uttering a word. The crowd rolled with laughter. The actor's neck was extended and his shoulders hunched in extreme effort. He was intensely frightened, but tried to maintain a "cool" front, and daringly presented himself as the "spokesman" for the motley group.

A second actor, Martial Arts, wore a half-mask that left his mouth exposed. Martial Arts turned on the crowd repeatedly, flaunting his prowess and skill. He patted Coward Flapping-Jaws on the back, explaining to the audience that Coward Flapping-Jaws was indeed capable of performing certain ritual duties.

"But this guy's got a problem. He can't control himself when the Holy One's around." His manner of speech was crass and the audience roared. By now, the musicians had joined in the laughter, fully absorbed in the Topéng hijinks.

Coward Flapping-Jaws began his frustrating attempts at speaking and finally succeeded in gaining control of his vocal cords. "Where's the rest of the crew?" he whined, his voice tearing to a high, uncontrollable pitch. "Maybe demons got them, maybe there's been an accident. That Drunk forgot to make the offerings. *Aduh, aduh, aduh,* eeeee, eeee, it's going to ruin the ceremony a, a, a, and, and, and . . ." His mouth continued flapping as he lost his voice.

The third actor sulking in the background wore a full-face Demon mask, with bulging eyes, receding brow, and gaping mouth packed with exaggerated teeth and fangs; frizzy tendrils of hair hanging down over his red-and-white-striped costume brushed his knees.

Released into the spectacle of celebration, the three wild actors seemed totally transformed from the troupe on the backstage *balé.* I wondered which one of these creatures was Kakul.

The Penesar and Kartala had exited unnoticed. Apparently, one of them had changed masks and reentered into the confusion as a Crass Official. His snarled-lip half-mask, with a single protruding tooth, was imposing. He stomped into the mêlée, hands on his hips, and took command of the crew. With a loud, rasping voice and an abrupt, elaborate wave of his arm, he commanded the actors into absolute silence.

Crass Official turned to the audience and began a seemingly endless narrative that elicited "oohs" and "aahs." The *gamelan* played a faint rhythmic melody to accompany Crass Official's message. The other actors, silent and frozen in place, began to move again, and Martial Arts unleashed himself into a ranting improvisation. He preened behind Crass Official. The *gamelan* picked up Martial Art's lead as he continued in unabashed adoration of his own strength. Crass Official turned slowly in annoyance to witness the shameless display, and with a flamboyant command, signaled the *gamelan* to stop. Only a few keys jangled.

Crass Official addressed Martial Arts. "This is incredible! You must be crazy to think that you stand any chance against the superior forces of the Mighty Ones!"

Martial Arts responded to the challenge by jabbing at Crass Official, but missed his mark each time. Martial Arts then turned to kick and nearly lost his balance. The two actors staged the mock—and mocking—battle so convincingly that when Coward Flapping-Jaws joined them, their joking was barely audible above the peals of laughter from the audience. The music spurred them on. They circled each other with such speed that they began to blur. They shifted pace. Then, suddenly, the *gamelan* changed and the actors' movements became slow and heavy. Their gestures seemed suspended. Coward Flapping-Jaws flapped on in silence as Martial Arts and Crass Official bantered and argued gracelessly about the etiquette of the ceremonies. A solo *gangsa* played a trivial accompaniment.

Martial Arts finally retreated in exhaustion and sat on the sidelines. The *gangsa's* melody diminished as Crass Official returned to lecturing the audience.

At the top of the steps, the Drunk that Coward Flapping-Jaws had mentioned rocked against the split gates. He steadied himself against one of the altars, then staggered down the steps into the arena.

"What's all this talk about work?" he sloshed.

Crass Official lost all patience. "You lazy, no-good low-life!" he yelled. "If you hang around here, we'll be threatened by some kind of evil force for sure."

"Where's the *arak?*" asked the Drunk.

The Demon roused itself. Crouching beside a small tree, its neck extended toward the action, it had observed every encounter in total concentration. Occasionally lifting its arms to its waist, it drew deep breaths, then relaxed, sinking into a slight bend of anticipation. These slow movements created a menacing tension between the four comedians and the solitary creature on the outskirts of the arena.

Coward Flapping-Jaws and the Drunk slunk off toward the tree where the Demon lurked in the shadows. Unaware of its presence, they danced in euphoric abandon to the lively rhythms of the *gamelan,* finally collapsing against the tree, and appeared to doze off while still standing. The music slowed and Crass Official hunched abruptly as if revealing guarded secrets. His eyes checked the action on each side to make sure everything was safe. He brought his hands together and continued. A small gong repeated in the background.

The audience gasped and whispered: the Demon slunk toward the Drunk and Coward Flapping-Jaws. It approached the two heedless souls slowly, each step weighted heavily, sinking and then rising as if dredging a swamp. It advanced, shaking its elongated, extended fingers, raising its arms in huge alternating arcs as it prepared to enfold the Drunk and Coward Flapping-Jaws in an inescapable web. Several villagers squealed, but the inevitable was about to occur.

The Drunk stretched, absent-mindedly poking the Demon. Turning slowly as he felt the Demon's long tendrils on his hands, he realized his situation, and instantly flung himself around Coward Flapping-Jaws, who awakened with his jaws flapping out of control. He tried calling for help, but could not muster so much as a squeak. He flapped in silence as the Demon detoured and headed for higher ground: toward Crass Official, who, completely unaware of the impending attack, continued speaking to the audience.

Releasing himself from the clutches of the Drunk, Coward

Flapping-Jaws finally managed a meek *"aduh,"* which he rallied into a warning shriek, "AAAA-DDD-UUUUUU-HHHHHH!" He began running around the courtyard in a panic. Crass Official spun around and threw his hands into the air just as the Demon was about to sink its fingernails into his neck. Crass Official shook the Drunk, who was now paralyzed with fear, and convinced him and Coward Flapping-Jaws to escape from the treacherous beast. They ran in futile circles around the courtyard. Martial Arts fled the scene in an instant.

The Demon, threatening with its sharp claws, chased after the remaining crew in labored steps. Hair flying wildly, feet lifting high, fingernails flashing in the glow of the lamps, it projected an eerieness full of latent humor. It jumped around suddenly and faced the audience, threw its head back, and poured out full, deep, sonorous laughter. Then it was silent—another flash of the nails, hair whirling in the echoing laughter.

The audience gasped. The power of this brute seemed greater than the human force of all the villagers combined. Children held on to each other, backing away from the arena, and squirmed in their parent's arms. Who possessed this force? I wondered. The creature seemed so gigantic, yet I realized it was actually little over five feet tall. The head, the hair, the extended fingernails, and the pendulous rags all added to its bizarre fierceness. I shivered, feeling both attraction and revulsion. The wind stirred. A cloud momentarily obscured the moon. Candles flickered.

Time seemed frozen in the Demon's reign of power. Crass Official huddled behind one of the flower altars, his fate uncertain as the Demon resumed its pursuit, and then screamed, seeking desperately to be rescued. The Drunk and Coward Flapping-Jaws, spiritless to the core, scampered through the gates. A stray dog chased after them. The Demon shook its arm a final time and appeared to leap the length of the courtyard when suddenly a huge Green Bird swooped through the gates, landing in front of the Demon. Behind the Bird, a Masked Raja appeared, his sword drawn. The music quickened. The Demon, startled, immediately turned away from

Crass Official and advanced toward the Green Bird, which beat its shieldlike wings, clacked its beak, jumped from side to side, and attacked the Demon in a mad frenzy.

The Demon retreated. The Masked Raja assisted the Bird in combat. Together they chased the Demon around the stage, the Raja brandishing his sword, while the Green Bird, with wings spread full, attacked with its beak. The now wild *gamelan* accompanied the attack in cacophonous precision. The Green Bird, flanked by a suddenly brave Crass Official, drove the Demon up the steps, through the gates, and out of the courtyard.

Screams and laughter from the crowd subsided as the music yielded to soft, slow-paced tinkling. The Penesar and the Kartala returned into the arena and humbly addressed the Masked Raja. The Raja conveyed his thoughts through the voice of the Penesar, commanding that preparations for the ceremonies continue now that the evil spirits had been driven from the vicinity.

But just as the audience had settled into the relaxed exchange between the Penesar and the Masked Raja, two more masked characters leaped through the gates, descending into the arena. Nervous Stutter and Impatient Lisp teased the Penesar and Raja. The Raja exited discreetly and left the Penesar and Kartala to restore order. As they instructed Nervous Stutter and Impatient Lisp in manners of the court, they were interrupted by the entrance of another masked character, Harelip. Uproarious laughter broke out in the audience as Harelip, Impatient Lisp, and Nervous Stutter all tried to speak at once. Impatient Lisp silenced his comrades and broke into silly, unrelenting laughter.

Again the laugh; was this Kakul, too?

Unable to follow the Penesar's detailed instructions, Harelip ran in circles, followed by his sidekick, Impatient Lisp, who yelled insults at Nervous Stutter. They bragged of their sexual prowess, their adventures, their devotion, and the laughter became fused with the banter. Dominating their laughter was that same shrill high peal, repeated over and over.

Harelip disappeared, and in his place, through the gates, came Silent Fool with a Limp. Then Nervous Stutter turned into a Clumsy Princess with crude hand movements. The forced smile of her homely mask attracted Fool with a Limp. After a brief *pas de deux* the couple exited arm in arm and immediately returned, transformed into Feeble Constipated Complainer and Gossipy Old Man.

"*Béh*," said Gossipy Old Man, scowling. "Did you see that Clumsy Princess dancing with the Fool?"

"*Aduuhh!*" groaned Feeble Constipated Complainer. "*Aduuhh!* Who can be interested in such elevated matters?"

The audience howled at each pun on unmentionable parts and functions of the body.

Embarrassed by this turn in the crowd's attention, the Penesar tried to repeat the ceremonial instructions, which he addressed to no one in particular. Finally he recruited the Kartala for the closing rituals.

But the jokes became more bawdy, and the laughter more raucous, and the characters continued to appear and disappear and transform before my eyes. The shrill laugh reverberated over the racing metallophones, the intensity of the gongs, the noise of the audience—shrill and high as if the wind itself were laughing. I felt intoxicated from the blur of action; my ears rang with tinkling and gongs and the jangle of the *gamelan*. Everyone seemed to accept the confusion of characters. The pitch increased, the lamps around the courtyard gleamed intensely, the incandescent colors of the actors' costumes shone like the explosive burst of an extinguished comet. Then suddenly the actors exited through the gate one final time, the laughter echoing in their wake. The Topéng performance was over. The music stopped.

The villagers stood up at once. Chatter and gossip and criticism and glee filled every conversation.

". . . and KAKUL!" exclaimed a small child.

"Remember when Kakul did this?" another child exclaimed as he demonstrated a huge leaping movement.

"And remember when Kakul did this?" said a little girl with a comical gesture. Listening with much curiosity, I wondered which one was Kakul. Everybody else seemed to know. I wanted to find out.

I tried to get back to the makeup *balé* before the actors left, but the crowd was too great. People were moving out of the courtyard toward the inner temple area where the priests' ceremonies were taking place. By the time I could approach the split gates, the kerosene lamps had been removed and the courtyard was empty except for the palm fringes and flower offerings, which shimmered faintly in the moonlight. It was only a few hours before dawn. I walked home through the rice paddies. The moon began to descend. The melody of frogs croaking in the irrigation stream caught my attention and I sat down on a stone to listen. A tinkling of bronze keys: first one, two, three, four, then all together, then silence, followed by the call of a frog downstream. A loud, solitary echoing. Then total silence.

Kakul's masks

KAKUL THE DANCE MASTER

I did not hear Kakul's name again in the months after the celebration at the Pura Dalem. Life continued in the usual way. I photographed daily ritual offerings, daily sweeping, twice-daily bathing, end-of-the-season cricket matches, preparation of the harvested rice, and replanting of the newly flooded *sawahs*. The sound made by women pounding rice was an ever-present musical accompaniment on dry hot days. Several villagers who worked the nearby fields had just delivered the last of the harvest into Ketut's family compound. Clear skies were especially valuable now, since the already stored crop could only be dried when the clouds lifted and the trade winds stirred everyone into bustling efficiency. On those days, the courtyard was jammed with tiny bundled sheaves drying on mats.

Leonard Pitt, the mime artist from the United States, had engaged a teacher in the village of Mas and I spent much time photographing his Topéng lessons.

The teacher had a reputation as an exceptional performer, but proved to be an inadequate instructor. At the beginning of each lesson, he quickly demonstrated the Prime Minister's entire pantomime, then seated himself in a corner of the *balé* where the lesson took place and motioned for Leonard to begin. But each step, effected by a complex pattern of impulses in fluid combination, was overwhelming for any novice. These impulses formed the continuity of the dance sequence, and knowledge of what motivated them was essential for the actor in order to communicate the character mask's archetypal. My photographic records of the lessons only showed a Westerner struggling through routines that were in conflict with his training and temperament. Attempts to translate the teacher's directions also proved futile. He stomped about, muttering a stream of Balinese incomprehensible to both Leonard and me. He pointed with flying gestures and threw tantrums regularly. His high-caste poverty was not ennobled by his sanctimonious attitude. Leonard would point to his hands and gesture as if to say, "Are these movements correct?" or to his feet: "Is this the right stance?" I searched through a pocket dictionary in an attempt to assist communication, but since the book contained only the basic Indonesian and no Balinese words, most of the time we resigned ourselves to using ineffectual sign language.

The dance instructor remained unimpressed. Eventually, in exasperation, he abandoned all attempts to communicate and "went away," sitting silently and staring off as the "lesson" progressed. After several weeks of this sort of frustration, the lessons became rote exercises, with silence the usual protocol for instruction. We were at an impasse.

Leonard, a true cosmopolitan, took solace in the superior blend of the local coffee. Strategically seated at Jero Arsa's *warung* in the center of Peliatan, he established an afternoon ritual of watching the rain. In this position, he remained quite dry and perfected the passing of empty time in the graceful manner of the Balinese. One rainy afternoon, I saw him share a coffee break with a young Balinese man who was giving an animated performance—of what, I did not know exactly, but it was formidable indeed. As I approached, I could hear that they were speaking in English.

"Well, you know," said B., the young Balinese, "I went to Australia and made so much money designing for the garment industry that when I returned to Bali, I decided to settle down in style and leisure. . . ."

His manners were theatrical, a delicate melding of entrepreneur and actor. He stroked his shag-cut hair with the thumbnail of his right hand. The two-inch long nail confirmed his new status. Certainly, it seemed, he had never planted rice in the paddies.

He continued in perfect English, "So I built this fantastic house, started exporting Balinese art, and now I've opened a boutique. I plan to go to England and meet my associates. Then—who knows?—on to an American tour, maybe."

He tossed his head in my direction, the shaggy hair falling perfectly into place.

"It will be fantastic! I plan to dance on this tour, and of course I want to show the traditional style—only what is authentically Balinese."

He adjusted the collar of his elegant black and white polka-dot silk sport shirt. With all his sophistication he seemed very excited about these new enterprises, and squirmed and giggled in childlike glee.

"I'm studying with the master of the classical dances—Kakul. He's fantastic! Like this"—the young man made several small movements. "He changes in an instant from a demon into a feeble man; from an enticing old woman into a high priest. His knowledge of movements is vast, his interpretations and improvisations are intensely dynamic, his characterizations and timing impeccable. His fame as a teacher is undisputed. He farms during the day and is a fancier of fighting cocks; and in the ritual performance he becomes the wizard of Topéng!"

B. jumped up and down now, improvising speeches as he assumed postures with arms outstretched, fingers extended in wavelike motion, then collapsed in laughter.

He sipped his *kopi* and continued: "Kakul performs the sacred Topéng Pajegan. He is famous for the satirical interpretations of the Topéng performed by his five-man troupe. He dances Gambúh, the classical adventure epics of the hero Panji. He sings the Arja romances and choreographs Warrior battles. And because his knowledge of these traditional forms is united with a wondrous playfulness, I'm amazed that he still teaches in such a disciplined way. Really," B. said, breathless, "you must come with me to my lessons!"

B. checked his wristwatch and excused himself, as he had an appointment at two o'clock. Leonard made arrangements to attend B.'s lessons the next day, and we waved goodbye to B. as he took off on his motorcycle toward the small market town where he lived. Leonard and I ordered another *kopi* while we considered B.'s pitch.

When I saw Leonard several days later, he enthusiastically told me that he had decided to study with Kakul. Each lesson produced fascinating stories about his new teacher. Every morning Kakul constructed shell crowns for the Baris headdress. Then, as a form of etiquette, he insisted on drinking *kopi* before the lesson. Besides creating a congenial mood, this small bit of time gave Kakul an opportunity to entertain the neighboring children with Topéng antics. His own children, all expert dancers in their own right, frequently arrived unannounced and participated in the criticism and instruction.

Kakul's three-year-old grandson already knew the dance that Leonard was straining to learn.

I decided to resume photographing the lessons, and one clear day I went to Batuan, Kakul's village. In the morning, the *bémos*, which were bound for the capital city of Denpasar, were full of women taking their wares to the district market in Sukawati, just south of Batuan. Several loaded *bémos* passed us before we finally decided that there was no alternative but to hop onto the back of an already jam-packed vehicle, which we did. Then four women, who had apparently completed their morning business, unloaded their parcels at the first crossroads and all the passengers stepped out; after the baskets were removed, Leonard and I found seats on one of the benches. Inside the *bémo,* dim light revealed a sea of faces: young children going to school, prim and scrubbed, all carrying satchels; women vendors, wearing brightly colored towels wound around the top of their heads. They spit red betel juice out the back of the *bémo.* They talked about market prices, complained about inflation (especially in the price of cigarettes), joked about Leonard's crunched, elongated body and curly red hair, and flicked eyebrows in secret communication to me.

A government official was sandwiched between a Balinese man and one of the market women. He was hunched in his seat and had fallen asleep, his chin resting on his chest. He rocked back and forth as the *bémo* jostled through the village of Mas. Completely unconscious of the activity in the vehicle, he began drooling. Everyone ignored him at first, continuing with heated conversations about economics punctuated by gossip and jokes. As other passengers got on, the official became more and more hunched over until it seemed his head would fall onto his stomach, and he drooled in a continuous stream. Some of the people began to laugh, covering their mouths in embarrassment, yet amused by his predicament. Finally, the laughter could not be contained. No one bothered to wake the official: any public loss of control is met with the same reaction—embarrassment and enormous amusement at the expense of the victim's self-esteem. The official drooled all over his lap and down the leg of his pants. After he was suffi-

ciently disheveled, the man seated at his side did wake him, and pointed out his situation. Thoroughly humiliated, the official frantically wiped his lap as the other passengers, now blasé and in control again, reverted to their own conversations and enjoyed their secret joke.

A young Balinese man dressed in Levi jacket and jeans wore a wristwatch that read four o'clock. Next to him was another modern Balinese, whose watch read eleven o'clock. Leonard's precision Seiko read 7:43.

We paid the money-taker just before a bend in the road, and jumped off the back of the *bémo* at the intersection to the village of Batuan. The path to Kakul's house wound down some steps and alongside an irrigation stream. People bathed nonchalantly; geese swam by. The tree-covered path opened up across a bridge. It continued on through the small neighborhood marketplace active with local women who shopped, bartered, gossiped, laughed, and played cards during lulls in business. One of the vendors sold flower petals for offerings. She also stocked local perfumes and healing pastes, which she applied to a customer. The land continued past several *warungs* situated at the crossroads and turned toward Kakul's family compound.

Once inside the narrow entrance gates to Kakul's compound, the path turned abruptly in to the inner courtyard, which was constructed in typical Balinese fashion. Diagonally opposite the compound's entrance a small garden area in the northern corner, oriented to the Gunung Agung, was enclosed by tall flowering trees and bushes and a low stone wall. Even from a distance of thirty feet I could see gardenia bushes, a frangipani tree, and an assortment of orchids and other tropical flowers.

A *taksu balé,* laden with offerings, was ringed by ancestor shrines—eight of them, a formidable presence. Carved stone bases supported tiny wooden boxes that concealed relics associated with ancestor worship. A figure of Cili, made of Chinese coins with holes in the center, was elegantly poised in the overhanging black palm-thatch roof of the main shrine structure.

Leonard and I waited for Kakul to arrive. We sat on a *balé* drinking the *kopi* Kakul's wife served. She explained that Kakul was still in the rice paddies, and then abruptly disappeared. Three laughing women carrying long bamboo poles walked into the compound totally absorbed in their own conversations. Their sarongs were old and faded but still beautiful; the pattern of the batik was visible and alive. Their breasts were scarcely covered by towels draped over the shoulders. They went to the back of the kitchen *balé,* still laughing, their movements vigorous and relaxed, and returned with Kakul's wife. The group crossed the courtyard to the granary. One woman climbed the ladder and removed several bundles of rice. Another carried the rice into the outer courtyard, and spread it out on a mat. Then they began to pound. Their bodies, moving in gentle undulations determined by the impact of the long bamboo pestle, depicted the power underlying an archetypal dance posture. The voices continued as counterpoint to the pounding of the rice. Kakul's wife carried the rhythm and set the pace. The others improvised. And the conversation continued. They let the towels fall and worked barebreasted in the morning heat.

In the distance I heard the faint jingle of a wooden cowbell; hollow and weak at first, it grew louder and louder until it became part of the rice-pounding symphony. A small figure

entered the pasture next to the area where the women were. He was leading a deerlike cow into the compound. He was very small, yet neither his size nor the mud-caked feet and the cow behind him could detract from the character that the lines in his face revealed. I did not recognize him.

His face came alive when he spotted Leonard and me on the porch. It was as if the anonymity of the thousand-year ritual of bringing in the cow from pasture had dissolved in an instant of recognition. Time and personality returned, and Kakul, the actor, was on.

He approached Leonard with eyes shining and betel-stained teeth gleaming bright red. Standing on tiptoes, he gave

Leonard a vigorous pat on the shoulder, then turned to me and laughed the deepest, longest, most wonderful laugh I had ever heard. He turned back to Leonard and pointed at me. He poked Leonard in the ribs, and laughed again, throwing his head back and folding his arms in front of his chest. Then, flipping his eyebrows in my direction and nodding his head in a seductive manner, he seemed to be speaking without words.

Leonard explained that I was a photographer, and asked Kakul for permission to photograph the dance lesson. Kakul exclaimed, *"Aduuuh!"* and rushed to bathe, reappearing in no time wearing a snazzy sport shirt. He insisted that I take his portrait.

The dance lesson was to be held in the shrine garden. Kakul led the way, his sarong entirely at ease with the bright modern geometric-patterned shirt. He deposited a flower offering on a miniature *balé*, explaining that it was a resting place for visiting ancestor spirits. At the frangipani tree behind one of the shrines, Kakul selected the fullest blossom—very carefully stripping away the leaves and stem until only the flower remained—then inserted this vibrant orange flower as a crown in the front of his hair. He sat at the base of the largest shrine and, by striking the first three notes of a melody on a *gangsa*, announced the beginning of Leonard's Topéng lesson.

The lesson was long and intense. When Kakul was not playing the instrument, he sang the Prime Minister's melody while standing in front of Leonard, demonstrating the posi-

tion of arms, legs, feet—of every part of the body. He would move behind and manipulate Leonard's body, molding him like clay, bending his knees and vigorously raising his shoulders until they reached his earlobes. The scene was not without humor as Kakul mocked Leonard's attempts, moving back and forth between Leonard's greatly overstated gestures and the minute insect-like movements necessary to convey the power of the Prime Minister's mask.

"If you don't assume the correct posture, you'll never make a connection with the Spirit of the Mask," Kakul said. "All your movements must be focused to portray the Prime Minister's true character." Kakul again interrupted the music and demonstrated: "Like this: at the designated moment, the Prime Minister must acknowledge the entrance of his King."

Kakul raised his left eyebrow and, with an acutely penetrating gaze, contracted the muscles surrounding the spinal column at the back of his neck, then sank into a posture of readiness, his feet pressing firmly into the ground, isolating the earth's strength. He gained control of it, raised it up into his eyes, and directed it out through his vision to connect with the fanlike extended fingertips of his outstretched left hand. He rotated the wrist of his left hand, transferring his submissive gaze onto the right hand and beyond it toward the presence of the King. Then, rapidly raising his left arm, using the elbow as a lever, he resolutely shifted the entire upper portion of his body, further heightening this posture of attentiveness.

"Remember, these impulses originate from your stance and are directed by the back of the neck. They are all controlled with a small but total exertion. If the movements are too large, the mask will not be convincing. The power must be contained from within."

Kakul began a fast-paced improvisation of various Topéng dance styles. Children ran in and out of the garden, watching intently, joking among themselves at Leonard's frustration, and imitating Kakul's antics.

"Each mask has its own drama," Kakul said as he encouraged Leonard's eyes into an exaggerated stare. "But even before the mask is worn, the actor must develop the character through posture, gesture, and breath."

Kakul assumed the role of the Dalem, dancing so slowly and with such grace that time, as we know it, seemed to be transformed: as if celestial winds moved through him to become the dance itself.

"After you have perfected these subtleties, you may improvise to a certain extent, but you must remain within the boundaries of the traditional choreography. In Topéng, the emphasis is on realism, which increases the force of our ancestral teachings. The Topéng must be understood even by the smallest child."

Kakul posed with right hand outstretched, pointing his index and middle fingers, and then flicking the gesture back toward his body with his wrist.

"You must obey my instructions!" he bellowed in the authoritative voice of the Prime Minister.

"Of course, while you're wearing the solid mask of the Prime Minister, you'll never say this in words, the Penesar will speak for you, but the urgency of this message must be expressed in your gesture or else the interpreter's voice will be weak! Whatever is expressed in your posture will be released in the gestures of your hands. If these gestures are not utilized, especially by those characters who perform at the beginning of the Topéng, then there is no language. And it is the language of gesture that conveys meaning through movement."

Leonard followed these instructions with concentration, using all his rational powers to muster the necessary control. He exerted enormous effort, but the visible results only revealed the struggle.

Kakul braced himself against Leonard's back and tried to get him to bend more at the knees. "You can't understand the power of this dance with your head alone," Kakul insisted. "You must lower your center." He began a lilting demonstration of Panji, the hero in the Gambúh, a chronicle play that is performed without masks. After the interlude he smoked a *kretek.*

"An actor who knows the Gambúh can embellish his Topéng characters with many ancient movements. You see, Gambúh gestures are exacting, because the dancer is restricted to expressing intricate poetic songs that create the rhythm of the drama. The emphasis is on abstract beauty, on the slow-motion extensions of the many qualities of time. *Halus.* But in Topéng, rhythm is strictly determined by using gesture and language to make ancient times live in the present. Each language, spoken or sung, corresponds to its own historical period and gives the Topéng drama varied texture and timing. The dancer must interpret this structure with a precise use of gesture.

"In any case, we won't bother with these details until you've found a mask that suits you. The lesson is over for today. Let's go to the mask-maker's; it's nearby."

Kakul demonstrating the refined movements of Topéng Dalem

Baris postures

I Madé Regug

"*Béh!*" he roared at the diminutive Kakul. "I'm so eager to do this story that I've lost my concentration for mask-making. We've got to arrange time to study the manuscript with a priest. In the meantime, I must return to working on the new Dalem mask."

Regug carefully indicated the subtle detail of the Dalem's radiant expressions. "Notice this, if you will. The tranquility of the refined eyes. The broad forehead, which will bear the stone of a third eye as a symbol of wisdom. This is the mask of moral strength; of reverence and mercy—the Prince of White Magic and the Keeper of the Soul." He inspected the interior shapes. "I've worked on this one mask for over two months already. It's the most difficult to execute with my limited knowledge. Sometimes I spend all day carving the position of the eye; the eyes must be focused from any position as the mask turns with the movement of the actor's head. I must be careful to make the gaze demure yet powerful. But my hands tire quickly, my spirit fades, and it becomes necessary to put this most holy mask back into the sack."

He handed the mask to Kakul, who, in the Topéng overture, performed the Dalem's dance. Kakul held the mask aloft, his palm resting behind the Dalem's brow. With terse, exacting rotations of his wrist, he moved the mask—it became alive.

Regug marveled, "*Béh,*" feeling pleasure and awe at the visage of the mask. "Once I fell asleep and the voice of my master spoke to me, reminding me of the sacred tree near the burial grounds. He described the roots of this tree making contact with the spirits of the ancestors—taking sustenance and guidance from them. When the tree was full of the wisdom of the ages, it became holy. The tree was cut down and the core divided into blocks, which, in turn, became the masks that my master made.

"My master's voice faded; I woke very startled and inspired," Regug confided. "I looked at these blocks, all hewn from the same tree, and continued my work with the reverence necessary to complete the Dalem's eyes."

I Madé Regug, the mask-maker, also performed in Kakul's five-man Topéng troupe. Regug's strong voice and stature made him a natural for the role of the Penesar, for which he was well known. When he spotted Kakul, he grabbed him by the arm and started to discuss a new story from the Chronicles of the Dynasty in Sukawati.

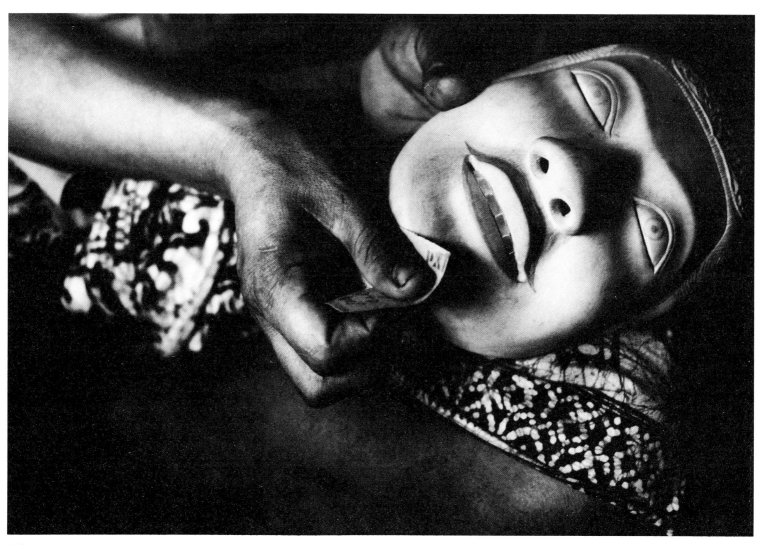

Dalem mask

Meanwhile, Kakul had found a Prime Minister's mask. He chuckled as he pressed it against Leonard's face. "Now, you are no longer who you think you are."

The next day, Leonard rehearsed with his new mask. Kakul called out a word: *"Tutup!"*

Up to this time, I had translated the Indonesian words that Kakul spoke in accompaniment to the dance's subtle movements. But we were still dependent on Kakul's demonstrations. Now Kakul had instructed Leonard to "cover," even though the mask already covered his face, closing off his mouth and leaving only small pinholes at the nose and narrow slits under the eyes. Leonard paused in the middle of a step to consider the implications.

Kakul pointed to Leonard's nose and repeated, *"Tutup!"* Not able to demonstrate, Kakul explained: "This expression is only for Topéng. During certain movements, you will take in a breath, raise your energy, and close your nose and all the openings of your body. Then, no evil spirits can enter while you are addressing a character of higher status."

Kakul giggled, becoming playful, then demonstrated one of the most distinctive and difficult expressions of Balinese dance: *kedis kelepuk,* a movement of the Gambúh.

"The huge owl sits in a tree in the forest until just before dawn; then, unexpectedly, it wakes up and utters, 'PUK.' "

Kakul released the haunting sound three times. At each utterance, he extended his neck forward slightly, then receded, his head bobbling gently from side to side, as if isolated on the top vertebra. Coming slowly to a stop, the "bird" was once again silent.

"Enough of this bird business. The Dalem must be able to soar to the heights on wings pure and swift. Nervous Stutter scratches and pecks like a clucking hen, but *you* must perform only the basics! Otherwise, you'll be confused and your postures will appear affected but without strength. Look at your feet!"

Kakul pointed at Leonard's feet accusingly and tapped on them with his mallet as Leonard passed the base of the shrine where Kakul sat. He stopped the lesson, asking Leonard to name various parts of the body in English. Kakul repeated each word: "Elbows, feet, toes." He leaped wildly, dissolved into laughter, then grasped Leonard's arm and emphatically declared, "POKOK! First, you establish a relationship to the earth, a foundation. Plant your feet and feel them extend down. Your whole body is the root that will grow from the core up toward the heavens. You must be able to draw your expression from those depths. Then you can dance with a mask if you please; you can shake the crown of a Warrior with fierceness; you can toss a gesture to the wind. Toes up," he shouted in English as he reached out to tap on Leonard's feet.

Kakul's instructions were compelling. I stopped photographing as I felt my feet twist into the ground. Suddenly, Kakul grabbed my hand, camera and all, directing me to walk around the courtyard.

"Walk!" Kakul imitated a drill sergeant as he led us. "Toes up," he insisted. "Feel your whole weight sink, toes up, toes up!"

Kakul giving a lesson

Leonard struggled to lower his center of gravity; my camera bounced on my chest. Kakul shouted with laughter at the sight of us. He approached me and said the Baris would be suited to my temperament and suggested that I begin to study immediately. He laughed again.

"If you come here every day, you must dance. You will learn the Baris. The Baris will teach you strength and expressions that must be internalized before you can dance with the mask. But now, you will walk only. This is the most important thing. First you connect with the source of your power; then the strength will be available as the tool of transformation."

Every day Leonard and I journeyed to Batuan by *bémo* for our lessons. In the morning, Kakul instructed several foreign students. First, Leonard studied the Topéng, and after him another American, Rucina Ballinger, and I studied the Baris solo. At noon, after attending their public school, two young Balinese girls from the nearby village of Blahbatuh arrived.

Kakul teaching the Baris

Kakul had choreographed a Baris duet for them as their basic instruction and because, traditionally, young girls did not perform this fierce, rigorous dance, much gossip circulated in the village of Batuan. But Kakul, who had taught his own daughter the Baris twenty-five years ago, ignored the gossip and stressed many kinds of intriguing interactions between the two young Warriors. During their lessons, he adjusted their postures to develop strength. He raised their arms until the girls created the illusion of formidable rank. He demonstrated powerful twirls, attacking and retreating. The young Warriors followed Kakul's lead, making gentle contact as comrades, battling with each other as foes, and circling to command an imaginary battlefield. They stopped and touched the center of their foreheads during a pensive interlude. Kakul encouraged them to magnificent displays of valor—their smiles

delicate and sweet, their gazes penetratingly fierce.

Kakul had many other students during this time. His courtyard was lively with discussions about dance and choreography; conversations were held in a spectrum of languages and in no language in particular. Vigorous expressions and gestures of arms, legs, and sometimes the entire body proved to be the most popular and entertaining language available to the diverse group that had sought out Kakul's instruction. Among Kakul's Balinese students were two boys who came for lessons late in the afternoon accompanied by their fathers. They studied the Baris, and usually arrived in time to watch the end of B.'s lessons. B. had arranged to study in midafternoon, so that he could conduct his business early in the morning—though the gossip in the village was that he was prone to laziness and enjoyed sleeping.

Competition between Kakul, the master of traditional style in Batuan, and T., a younger and more rebellious performer, grew to tasty proportions as far the the gossipmongers were concerned. Not only did the brothers of the young Balinese girls study with T., but rumor had it that T. was jealous of Kakul's popularity as a teacher. Aside from the intense competition, everyone seemed to have a definite opinion about the Baris duet that Kakul had created for the Balinese girls.

One day after my lesson, I went to have coffee at a *warung* on the main road a short distance from Kakul's compound, and there I overheard some men talking in resolute voices. Apparently, the controversy surrounding the girls' duet was not unprecedented: Kakul's daughter Dawan, who had achieved acclaim and notoriety as a young Baris dancer, was now performing the leading role of Panji in the classical Gambúh play, another traditionally male role. Even though there was no official restriction on the casting of this heroic character, who possesses the power to transform his sex, his species, or even his corporeal form at will—and even though Dawan was highly respected in the role, criticism of Kakul's daring innovations continued.

"How could Kakul do such a thing?"

"This sort of teaching is unnecessary and outrageous!"

"Completely useless."

"Foolish."

"A dangerous example, at best!"

"Kakul must be planning to start his own army!"

The gossipmongers laughed and continued speculating on the effects of Kakul's attitudes. Villagers returned from the fields, stopping for a glass of *arak*; children came to the *warung* on errands. Several hours passed unnoticed as other villagers joined in the banter.

Into this typically Balinese scene walked Sardono, a Javanese director and choreographer. He wore blue jeans, aviator glasses, and a Javanese work shirt. His straight black hair hung loose to his shoulders. He carried a motorized Nikon camera. As he sat down, I recalled the purpose of his visit to Batuan. Kakul had spoken of Sardono's involvement with Balinese theater: in the early 1970s, Sardono had worked with Kakul while creating a new Ketchak dance in the village of Teges. Now Sardono was reinterpreting the myth-legend Chalonarang, which was scheduled to tour Europe and several international theater festivals. Sardono's productions were noted for their fiery combination of traditional dance forms with modern theatrical methods. He ordered a glass of *brem*, and we began to talk about his work with Kakul. He spoke lucidly in English, carefully selecting each word.

"The Balinese have a keen insight into the power of the dance," he said. " 'The word must move,' Kakul has said. 'The sound must move.' So, suddenly he sat down in the Ketchak circle; and when all the people made the sound 'OM,' he made 'OOOOOMMMMMM,' like this. . . ." Sardono demonstrated, bringing his hands together at his heart and lifting both arms straight up past the top of his head, opening them as they reached their full extension.

"Do you mean to say that as everyone made the sound, he made the gesture?"

"Yes. Spontaneously. You understand? Kakul sat and made this movement. So when I saw this, I introduced it to the people of Teges village. They accepted the movement and still use it in their Ketchak performance."

"Did Kakul say the gesture had a meaning?"

"Not at all."

"Did you discuss it?"

"No."

"Then, it was irrelevant?"

"Yes, exactly. It happened that I asked Kakul to teach the basic Baris to my own troupe while I was at Teges. But soon after he'd begun, he suddenly stopped and said, 'Ah, forget it; it's better that I see what you have done.' "

"Was he open to your approach?"

"Yes, that is what I found fascinating. Kakul realized the potential of receiving something and then taking this mysterious thing and creating a new structure spontaneously."

"Do you find this unusual?"

"Yes, to be spontaneous, to be open, and to have the power to initiate communication!"

"What do you mean by 'initiate communication'? "

"We all have a tremendous potential for expression if we are open to all impulses. It is this kind of language that is the most universal." He paused to sip his *brem*. "For instance, Kakul's ability to perceive and to act simultaneously: he sees and takes the expression of the language, of the body, the feeling, and so forth—which, of course, is wider than just words—and with this awareness he is free of manner and persona. Do you understand? This is the basic attitude."

He elaborated. "From the time the Balinese are children, not only are they used to exploring the range of their emotional capacity but they are encouraged to do so. It may be because they live in a village. Balinese children do not have only one father and one mother but various fathers and mothers, and these relationships facilitate exploration." Sardono paused as some children ran into the *warung*. "Everybody here supports children when they feel shaky—family, siblings, other children, and adults in the village. Infants are never put on the ground before they can walk by themselves. Everyone takes turns holding them in their arms. There is enormous trust. Not too much patronizing, not overly taking care. The result is that the Balinese accept the wide range of the qualities of emotions from early childhood onward without jeopardizing their safety. In this way, children are a part of the larger society, with equal responsibility and equal play.

"Whereas, in so-called more sophisticated cultures, it seems that there is restriction very early: that if something happens, a judgment is made that an experience will not be 'good' for the child. In Bali, if we see a child learning dance and he makes an error, the teacher will scream and make a scene. It is considered, in more modern societies, that this will

"For myself, I do not work here as an individual or as a unique artist seeking self-expression. My expression, the form, is just the extension of the state of mind. So if a foreigner learns only the movements, it is nothing but empty movement."

"What do you consider to be the origins of this form?"

"It was after studying the Baris with Kakul, after working with him, after three months of experiencing the many rituals, basically not so strange to me as a Javanese, since our roots are in the same spirits, and after much study and discussion that I realized that this form originates in the *sanghyang*. It was during a performance of the Sanghyang Dedari that I saw the potential danger of entering into trance and that, because of this, people started praying; several men started making the sound 'chak, chak, chak, chak, chak.' Everybody who felt like joining in the spirit picked up 'chak, chak, chak, chak, chak,' and so long as the pattern of the voice was collective, there was no formality. This rhythm brought people into the deeper emotions. Actually, that is what is called in Bali *'Tat tvam asi'*: 'I am You and You are I.' "

"If you do not concern yourself with the style of the dance, what did you learn by studying the Baris and Topéng with Kakul?"

"I wanted to feel, to experience the quality of the emotion and the quality of the movement, instead of learning Topéng as a style or Baris as a dance. I feel that the Baris is a dramatic dance. It is dramatic in a sense that is different from the so-called drama of the modern theater. The drama is in the dynamic movements which the dancer makes visible at the exact critical point [of time and place] where the world of reality and the world of the supernatural or transcendental meet."

"Do you consider this a process of transformation?"

"Exactly. Instead of dramatization, it is a pure dramatic field."

"Is this the purpose, the goal of the drama?"

"Basically, you will find that there is really no goal, no result, because there is no ambition. We are still talking about a state of pure receptivity, an inner form. The root of this concept is within the temple ceremony. Suddenly, someone will

cause a traumatization in the child—thinking that it is not good to make children angry. But this expression is allowed to happen here; it is part of daily experience."

Sardono finished his *brem* and lit a cigarette. The village lanes were quiet now. I asked him if he thought it possible for a foreigner to learn the forms of Balinese theater and dance.

"There are two things here. The first is a specific thing: the form of the acting which is studied, a particular dance or gesture. The second is what lies under the form itself. That is, the order of the Balinese daily life."

"Do you think that it is possible for a foreigner to translate or assume this attitude?"

enter into trance. So, you know, this person is not one to have any ambition. It is not the goal, but it is what happens."

The afternoon was almost over. Sardono remained at the *warung*. In hopes of watching B.'s lesson, I returned to Kakul's house by way of a wide road that led through the center of the village. This road was considerably more traveled than the tiny footpath that meandered next to the irrigation canal along the eastern border of Kakul's *banjar*. Affluent villagers maneuvered their new motorbikes; less affluent ones rode bicycles.

Just at the intersection of the main road and the Pura Desa, the road split off to a sharp left and continued alongside the primary school. A short distance down this road, a large frog sculpture sat in front of the *balé banjar*—used, besides its regular functions, as the rehearsal hall of the "frog opera" and of the orchestra that accompanied the Gambúh play. Sometimes, on the occasion of a special festival, musicians gathered there with their four-foot-long flutes to serenade the dancers before the performance.

Several villagers met, exchanged greetings, and continued on their way. Men squatted gracefully by the intersection with their fighting cocks. Youngsters chased after a wretched dog. A very old woman sat behind a low table, selling crispy rice cakes and various kinds of dried fish. Her huge hands, callused by many years of work in the fields, did not prevent her from picking up each parcel with the utmost delicacy and precision. She had betel nut in her mouth and readjusted it constantly as her laughter displaced the gooey red ball. The men with their fighting cocks sat directly across the path from her stand and except for an occasional village woman who bought fish, she was the only woman in the area. Several days earlier, Kakul had told me she was the respected elder who led the Rejang now performed each evening in the Pura Desa. The contrast of the fighting cocks and the eloquent dancer, "disguised" as an old woman behind a fish stand, was startling. But as I pondered the logistics of remaining in Batuan to watch her performance or returning to Peliatan before nightfall, a slight rain began, and I was almost knocked over by a

motorcycle that sped by me. It was not until the Balinese rider abruptly brought the vehicle to a stop that I recognized him as B.

"Well, hop on!" he shouted, pointing to the seat. "I'll have to give you a ride now. If I stop to talk, I'll be late!" He continued mockingly: "And besides, you know Kakul, he'll probably scold me and charge me overtime."

He laughed as he revved up the motorbike, for we both knew that Kakul did not charge his Balinese students any fees. Then with great abandon he raced through the village, over stone embankments, through mud puddles, around corners, and into the entry of Kakul's compound.

Kakul was sitting on a *balé*, fastening flame-shaped shells onto a Baris crown. After cutting, filing, and carefully drilling a hole at the base of each shell, he threaded a short wire through the hole. Then he wound the wire around a tiny nail, giving the shell a spring action that would shake with the dancer's movements. Finally, he threaded the shell onto the frame of the crown. He was in a good mood as he greeted us, singing romantic melodies from the Arja romances and laughing as he responded to his own questions in a coy sweet voice. Kakul casually dismissed B.'s lateness and announced that he had canceled his lesson for that afternoon.

Kakul asked me if I would remain in Batuan for the Rejang. When I explained the difficulty in returning to Peliatan late at night, he laughed at my reasoning and invited me to live and study in his household. I was surprised by his spontaneous offer—flattered, but overwhelmed at the thought of obtaining official government approval to live outside the designated tourist accommodations. (Little did I know at the time the warmth with which Kakul would be received by the visa officials and the hospitality that they would extend to me because I was Kakul's student.)

As I returned in a *bémo* to Peliatan, a solid curtain of monsoon rain lashed against the vehicle while it passed through the village of Mas. The course of the monsoons seemed consistently to avoid the villages directly to the south of Peliatan. Sometimes a lonely motorbike traveler would stop at the crossroads in Peliatan seeking shelter from drenching rains, only to report that the village of Batuan was enjoying bright sunshine. This made Kakul's invitation all the more tempting.

By the time I arrived at the entrance to Ketut's homestay, the main road was flooded and the footpath barely visible under several feet of water. Great caution was necessary in walking to the *pondok,* as a minor slip would have left me in the middle of a slimy, muddy pool; the two-inch rubber soles on my sandals were not high enough to keep me from sinking with each step, and I clumsily lost one sandal as the suction pulled it into the earth. Fortunately, Ketut had left several marker stones, visible even during the flooding, to indicate the path, and I made my way to the *pondok* barefoot, mateless sandal in hand.

The lotus pond had flooded across the path, and the irrigation stream—if given several inches more rain—threatened to do the same. Water had already reached the first step of the *pondok,* and fungus had begun to invade my camera equipment in spite of all technological precautions. I consulted with Ketut about mobility during the monsoons; when he said it was difficult at best, and always messy, we concluded it would be best for me to move to Batuan.

Sheltered by an umbrella, I walked to the Puri Agung to visit Leonard, and found him sitting at his usual afternoon snack shop. He laughed at me for venturing out in such ghastly weather. Jero Arsa, the proprietor, agreed with him, saying that it was very uncivilized to be in such a hurry and not wait for the unpleasantness to pass.

The rain stopped; a bright clear sky appeared from behind the mass of rain clouds. I went with Leonard back to the Puri Agung. He was packed and ready to leave for the United States on the following day. The last glow of sunlight cast all colors in shades of gold.

Leonard left before dawn the next day, just ahead of another downpour that swept through Peliatan. That afternoon, I waited in the rain for a *bémo* to move my bags to Batuan. Finally managing to transport my equipment without becoming waterlogged, I arrived at Kakul's house, settled into the room next to the kitchen *balé*, and took the usual evening bath. Kakul was in the middle of an evening lesson with B. and did not want to be disturbed. B.'s performances had great fire, but his discipline was practically nonexistent, his movements full of bravura but sloppy in execution. B.'s concentration waned. Kakul called the lesson to an end and addressed me casually: "Have you bathed?" B. left, exhausted.

Only the sound of rain filled the dark compound. A small kerosene lantern illuminated the work *balé* where, for several hours, Kakul's wife had been creating offerings. The celebration of the Balinese New Year, Galungan, was still some time off, but offering-making was already in progress. Ibu sat draped in sarong and towel; she savored a grapefruit during a brief respite.

The next morning was sunny and clear enough for me to walk down a steep gorge through the paddies to a quiet spring-water bathing shrine. The view across the gorge to the newly planted *sawahs* was typical of the central highlands, carved out of water, governed by the water itself.

In the afternoon, the rains began again. Dawan and her eight-month-old son had come to Kakul's for a visit. With her small baby wrapped in a *selendang* supported on her hip, she sang one of Panji's tales in the poetic verses of the Gambúh. The sky continued clouding over, denser than the previous days. On another *balé* Kakul played a melody from the Topéng on a double-stringed *rebab*. Dawan passed the boy to his grandmother, who positioned his tiny hands into the stance of the Topéng Keras. Slowly, the boy turned himself to-

ward Kakul, who sat across the courtyard playing the haunting instrument.

Raising his tiny arms with fingers outstretched, without any prodding, he stood by himself, and while his grandmother hummed the Topéng melody, he began moving toward the music. Barely able to hold his body erect, not really capable of walking, he already had the attitude of the Topéng within him and danced in exquisite form. Dawan sang to the accompaniment of the yearning strings. Ibu caught the little dancer as soon as he reached the end of the platform and tickled and teased him with tender affection.

Now that I was a part of the activities in the family compound, my lessons began at seven o'clock in the morning. Kakul concentrated on the difficult movements related to the eyes and to changes in direction during the first part of the Baris—the wild part in which the Warrior establishes the attitudes of fierceness and courage. The strength required to execute even the tiniest movement was immense, and Kakul stressed the walk as the key to untapped energy. He pushed me closer to the ground, insisting that the knees bend more, that the legs assume a wider stance, at the same time lifting me up at the shoulders so that my elbows were on the same level as my neck.

"If this line is maintained, the power will surge through your entire body and seek release through quivering fingertips. But, if you weaken for an instant, fatigue will conquer and the Warrior will be defeated."

I was worn out by ten o'clock and took a nap during the late morning heat.

The girls from Blahbatuh arrived for their lesson. To Kakul's surprise, a younger brother of theirs, who studied with T., accompanied them. The younger brother's bold venture into Kakul's territory demanded a show of strength, and the boy immediately realized the error of his visit. Very embarrassed, yet obliged to maintain at least a semblance of courage, lest T.'s reputation fall, he started to dance while Kakul played the music on a small *gangsa*. The boy moved

with assurance, but his walk was bouncy, giving a comic over-tone to every movement. His legs were practically straight, so that when he tried to raise his energy, his efforts were in vain, and his eye movements only punctuated his frustration. He stomped around, his elbows falling, his face expressionless. At the conclusion of the first part of the dance, the children who had gathered in the courtyard imitated his crude movements. The boy asked to be excused, as he was now late for his lesson with T., and quickly ran out of the compound.

Kakul refused to comment, and instead focused on a new confrontation between the girl Warriors. He angled between them, explaining how they would have to stalk each other, cir-cling, until a clash broke out and one of them yielded and knelt before the other in deference to the victorious strategy.

The transitions were very complex: straight walks in parade fashion, changing to circular stalking, and resolved in an ab-rupt statuesque pose.

The lesson ended in the early afternoon, giving Kakul plenty of time to go to the Pura Dalem where a cockfighting arena was set up in counterpoint to the nightly Rejang. Kakul left with his fighting cock to attend the matches, already in progress.

The next day, Kakul was in a depressed mood because he had placed a bet on a losing bird. His honor and pride seemed more damaged than his pocket, for the bet amounted to very little. He decided to cancel my lesson, and suggested that we go to the village of Blahbatuh to make arrangements for the festival of their Pura Dalem, in which he had been invited to dance.

Kakul enjoyed his reputation. Word of his radical choreog-raphy had spread throughout the district; people in the *bémo* recognized him and talked to him about his students. They pointed at me, and were very curious to know which dance Kakul taught me. As soon as he mentioned Baris, they ex-claimed *"Béh!"* and insisted that I demonstrate at least a fierce expression. I was aware that my teacher's reputation was at stake—I furrowed my brow, flared my nostrils, and mustered up the sweetest smile imaginable. *"Béh!"* they responded again and expressed their admiration to Kakul for being able to teach, even to a foreigner, such subtle and exacting expres-sions. After this "test," everyone felt enough at ease to joke and tease; but Kakul, dressed in his formal white shirt and gray-flannel slacks, remained aloof.

Once in Blahbatuh, Kakul detoured to visit his old friend Ketut Rinda, another Topéng dancer who, with Kakul, had been a member of the group that had toured the world in the 1950s. "Pak" Rinda was respected for his wide knowledge of Balinese dance legend and mythological stories. He and Kakul discussed the progress of the Baris duet, which Ketut Rinda recognized as a brilliant creation although he himself adhered to a strict classical style. Then Kakul excused himself, explain-ing that he had to meet with the head of the village.

The *kopi* in the home of the head of the village was an exceptionally strong, pungent brew. Conversation increased the ambiance already established by the host's graciousness. Kakul complimented him; considering this a good sign, the host offered Kakul a *kretek,* which added the sound and smell of crackling cloves to the gathering. The negotiations began with brilliant style, and after what seemed the appropriate amount of time and discussion, the head of the village covered his empty *kopi* glass with a lid and announced the arrangements resolved.

Before the afternoon was over, just as the *bémo* arrived in Batuan, clouds descended onto the plains and broke into an angry downpour. The rain was intense and short lived, but that evening clouds hung low, concealing the almost full moon. No rain fell.

Like a warm blanket hovering over the village, the scent of night-blooming orchids filled the air. Kakul and I went to the Pura Desa to buy cigarettes. There the sounds of a hollow, languid, tinkling *gamelan* announced the performance of the nightly Rejang. Hundreds of young women, small girls, toddlers, and an occasional respected elder gathered under the *balé* in costumes of the most resplendent materials. In their hair the girls wore tiaras of frangipani buds, each bud inserted into a fuller one and cut into delicate strips, creating a blossom of intoxicating proportions. Pounded gold flowers in frangipani-like design embellished each headdress. Kakul walked over to the dancers, who stood at the west end of the twenty-meter-long *balé.*

As usual at the *warungs,* the voice of gossip shed new light on the performance. "Our favorite vendor is leading the Rejang," said a man who passed time at the popular intersection with his fighting cocks. He referred to the old woman who sold rice cakes opposite the rehearsal *balé* near the main road. "No one can match the delicacy of her dance."

"Or her grace," his companion added.

"Or the subtlety of her gestures," added another of the cockfighters.

"Or the power of her devotion," concluded the first man. "Too bad. The young women are so sloppy. They wave their arms, and make movements without conviction. How can we be assured of keeping the village purified if the future holds such attitudes?"

They shook their heads in agreement and went on to criticize each nuance of the previous night's performance.

"Tell me," said a man who had come to the Pura Desa from one of Batuan's twelve *banjars.* "Is it true that T. has beaten Kakul as the number one Topéng dancer of Bali?"

The others laughed, but continued the discussion in muffled voices. One leaned forward and whispered, "Kakul is the superior actor. His knowledge of classical forms is refined. His interpretations are sublime, and his voice is so engaging that everyone enjoys every sound he utters. But certain people will always look for a weakness, and Kakul must be careful to guard his *taksu* against black magic. T., no doubt, is the contender. His style is exhilarating, and we all need a boost now and again. I know people who think that the classical forms have lost their meaning. Besides, they've become boring to watch."

He leaned farther forward and admitted, "I myself think that Kakul is finished, but, don't get me wrong, he really made an impact during his time."

One of the men had turned his back to the gossipers in discreet rejection and was engaging the proprietor of the *warung* in conversation when the ground started to shake: a minor tremor echoed from the distant Gunung Agung. All the villagers ran into the open courtyard of the temple, beating the ground with sticks and laughing and shouting in contained hysteria. After several minutes the tremors stopped, and everyone returned to wait for the performance to begin. Occasional nervous titters, revealing deeply hidden fears, were quickly masked over by idle conversation.

The repetitive and hypnotic melody of the Rejang began without any distinguishing opening chords: one activity slipped into the next. It was like a meditation, each movement punctuated with the suspended lilt of an outstretched arm. Six parallel rows of dancers began to traverse the entire Pura Desa in a seemingly eternal slow-motion crossing.

At the head of the center row, the old woman dancer stood poised. She established the pace of the purification ritual, sweeping aside her train with distinct, fluid movements. She formed *mudras* at the appropriate interludes, hesitating only for an instant, allowing the sweetness to linger before returning to the journey ahead.

Her movements were restrained, exact, then quick—a flick of the wrist—and slow again, concentrated, her head still, her back straight, her eyes motionless yet clear. She lifted and swayed with each minute step. As she completed the cycle, she stood poised, breathing deeply several times. Her breath followed the rhythm of the music, and she began the cycle again, bringing her hands together to form the *mudra* in front of her chest. Sweeping her left arm up on one side, she lifted and swayed, again breathing the meditation, leading the lines, which grew longer and longer behind her until she had crossed the whole *balé*. She seemed to expand each moment, repeating and suspending the movements, until she faced the offering table in the darkness. A priest sprinkled her with holy

Rejang dancer

water and a priestess gave her an offering cake made of sweet coconut shreds and bright pink rice. Behind her the long rows were constantly replenished by the crowd of girls, who waited their turn at the back of the *balé*. Not until many hours later, far into the night, when the last row of girls performed the Rejang in a final crossing, did the purification ritual end.

The walk back to Kakul's compound was not quiet or dark. Even in the hours just before dawn, people with lanterns walked to the temple carrying offerings on their heads. The moon descended behind the paddies.

Despite the hour, Kakul gave a critique of the *gamelan* during the Rejang performance, insisting that the musicians did not concentrate; the melody meandered slightly, causing a

Kakul's grandson

general slack in the posture of the dancers. He demonstrated the dynamic relationship between the *pokok* stance and the upheld horizontal line—of the chest, shoulders, and arms—reminiscent of the *wayang*.

"First, the toes must be raised so that the tension of feet pressing into the earth creates a powerful contact with vital energies. The *pokok* gives all movement conviction! Then, the legs must bend deeply so that these energies can be drawn up into the body, and when this energy intersects the upheld line at the back of the neck, its power is transformed.

"In the Rejang, this upheld attitude sustains a balance within the meditation. Tonight, only the old woman maintained a unified 'Presence.' *Béh*, the younger dancers have no stature."

Kakul elaborated on the significance of this upheld attitude.

"In the Baris Pendet, if the line is not upheld, the devotional offerings which the Warrior holds in front of his heart will be presented in front of the stomach, and this is too embarrassing to even consider! And in the Baris solo, the upheld line increases fierceness. Without it the Warrior is weak, vulnerable, and evil may enter.

"But in the end, if the *taksu* is going to enter, a calmness and quiet must form in the breath, which is at the center of this dynamic."

Although Kakul demonstrated his point only briefly, his face was completely transformed. "In the Topéng Dalem, the foundations, the force, the line, and the tranquility have all been synthesized with such devotion that no effort is needed to communicate the power of the King. It is like the unseen wind, who stirs all things in continual passing."

Kakul became submissive to the directions emanating from deep within his soul. He raised an eybrow as he danced around the courtyard. His feet delicately but authoritatively brushed the ground; his arms served as graceful billows while he allowed his breath to move him through the dance. Day began to break. Kakul released himself from his reverie and walked off to his sleeping pavilion.

Several hours later, he awoke energized. "I've had a dream," Kakul said, before my lesson began. "During the dark-est part of a moonless night, I ventured into the forest and heard many unfamiliar sounds. One soft cry repeated over and over, 'Ki-kur-i-ku tooo-too.' Birds circled over my head. 'Too-too clil-clil.' Suddenly, as I approached the great Naya Sari tree in the inner sanctuary of the temple, a white temple pigeon, the Titiran, swooped down toward my head. 'Nki-nki-nkir.' I tried to catch it but did not succeed."

He seemed momentarily unlike himself, and "went away"; then in a split second he returned to explain the role of the eyes in the Baris solo.

"You must use your eyes to heighten your awareness of the stage. Your expressions must be intense; they must convey certainty. I cannot tolerate the sloppiness of a blinking dancer. 'Presence' is of utmost importance and must be unwavering. Open your eyes wider. Breathe deeper and release the breath through your palms and fingers."

He hunched behind me and wrapped his arms around my shoulders, straightening my back into precise alignment. Then he dashed in front of me and pointed to my eyes, "You must have wild eyes, *galak!* And sweet lips, *manis!*"

He continued to shout instructions: "I want to see fierce eyes and sweet subtle smiles—only then will you become provocative. Raise your eyebrow! Elbows up! Your wrists and elbows must be at the same level as the eyes. Remember, a flick of the wrist and the eyes move. You must refine your movements."

This rigorous session continued for several hours, until Kakul's wife brought *kopi*. I collapsed in exhaustion and Kakul went off to feed his cow.

The girls from Blahbatuh arrived for their lesson just as Kakul returned. He instructed them in the very slow walk of the second part of the duet, continuing to emphasize the attention that they must sustain toward each other, even when they were not in direct eye contact.

"If you sense each other's presence, the audience will interpret this as a kind of tension and will anticipate your combat and interactions. You will not just be seen as separate entities, but will create the intrigue of a political situation."

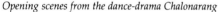
Opening scenes from the dance-drama Chalonarang

They practiced until sweat poured from their foreheads. Kakul bent their knees lower to the ground. He raised their arms, helping them to sustain the upheld line, and bent the hands back to accentuate their already angular posture. He sat down to smoke a cigarette while calling out the steps and instructing the girls to increase their awareness of the approaching foe. Or was it a comrade? Kakul introduced an element of doubt.

"These matters concern the Warrior's heart. We know it is a pounding heart, a brave and courageous heart, a heart full of the feelings of battle, and of life. But it is only the first step of the more hidden heart: of the attention, concentration, and passion of the devoted soul. You must understand this to the core before you can 'win.' Otherwise, the battle is lost, and the Warrior is lost."

He interrupted the lesson and walked to his sleeping porch, continuing to speak about performing in general: "Not only the gods express their appreciation for high devotion, but the audience itself benefits from such striving. It is the dancer's responsibility, and especially the Topéng dancer's, to communicate the teachings of the ancestors. The power of the mask, its spirit, will speak only if the actor is devoted and in a state of total receptivity. Then the words will come. Then the language of sublime movement is possible. When the dancer is in this state, the audience will be attentive, will learn, will prosper, and will continue to practice the teachings. Otherwise, all will be lost, the audience will fall asleep, or wander off to gamble, or leave the performance, or laugh the 'dramatic' actor off the stage. And so you must continue in earnest. That way you'll be able to compete and beat several of the lazier students who seek fleeting rewards." He laughed, explaining that it is very important to compete, but not to cause the exclusion of another dancer.

"You must feel the life, the flow from your heart, from your soul," he concluded, emphasizing a new movement with his eyes closed.

His favorite fighting cock jumped up onto the porch, and he put it on his lap, then continued teaching the new gestures. Occasionally, the tail feathers framed his face. His grace and the isolated beauty of each gesture were fascinating and awesome.

"I learned this *mudra*," he said, demonstrating it, "near the court of the old Klungkung palace from a powerful holy man who lived nearby. During that time, I taught dance to the children who lived in the palace, as well as others from neighboring districts. I am a common person, and the names of these gestures are long forgotten. I do not know their meaning either. But their power is not hidden from me: they express a sign of devotion, and confirm my intention to perform sacred ritual."

That evening, word circulated through the *banjar* that T.'s Chalonarang troupe had been commissioned to perform in a nearby village. I walked through a palm jungle and several rice fields to see the performance. Kakul stayed in Batuan to avoid any embarrassment or accusations of ill intent.

The drama was fleeting—each character entering and exiting with such haste that the dance was lost. Several old men who sat in front of the stage area left in the middle of the overture. As the play began, I turned and walked back to Batuan, stopping for cigarettes at the *banjar warung*. Gossip about T.'s performance had already begun.

"Too many fast movements meaning nothing."

"Weak voices."

After I arrived at his compound, Kakul became bored by my description of the performance and announced that he would teach me the Rejang.

"The two girls will dance with me at the celebration in Blahbatuh. Their brothers, who study with T., will also dance. For this reason, the performance will be seen as a competition, and since you are now considered to be part of my troupe, it will be necessary for you to compete also. It doesn't matter if

Chalonarang consults a spirit

you make a few mistakes. This will be a demonstration of courage. You must increase your strength and be brave. Right now, this is the most important attitude. But before this event, you must purify yourself by performing the Rejang, as an offering to my village."

He began to demonstrate the Rejang, slowly, with great concentration: lift and sway, a delicate balance, and a walk with sweeping grace. His every step was sure and strong, and as graceful as could be imagined.

"The pace must be exact, each gesture calculated but ef-

fortless. This is a moving meditation, a purification that seeks to merge with an eternal peace."

B. had not studied with Kakul for several weeks. His motorbike could be heard at the crossroads, turning away from Kakul's house. Apparently he had decided to study with T. At the *banjar warung* within sight of the crossroads, several of the men who had been watching B.'s new path busied themselves with speculation on his defection.

"I'm sure that he really wants to become a rich celebrity.

Jauk taunts the gamelan

You know that T. has gained great success as a brilliant *bintang baru.''* Everyone laughed at the pun: Bintang Baru, or New Star, is the name of the beer sold throughout Indonesia.

"Well, certainly B. won't learn anything about traditional dance there."

"Nobody really cares or pays attention to all those subtleties anyway."

"But those French people who come to visit T. commission performances for large sums of money."

"Yes, I know, but one of the servants told me that they only come to drink *tuak* and spend all their time talking with each other and that the performances are over in an instant, and nobody really watches them anyway!"

"Odd behavior!"

"Too bad. T. is really a brilliant performer in his own right, and his following among the Balinese is definitely growing larger."

The two men returned to sipping *kopi* and goading the owner of the *warung* to reveal more gossip about Kakul and his students.

The next day, Kakul's son Klub brought his drum to my lesson. The movements were now clearly linked to the beats of the drum, the fingers responding to this subtlety by leading the eyes in new directions. This precision of spirit fueled the fierceness necessary before the movements of attack and withdrawal: the attack, a culmination, and then a retreat to a composed stance of victory.

Kakul taught me a new maneuver, one of surprise and wonderment, which he called "to look under the umbrella." He used his hand as a visor, delicately tilting it above the crown of his head.

"OOOOOHHHH, who can be there? Aaaahh," he responded to his own question with reverent sweetness. "So it is You. . . . This is daring, full of awe."

Kakul taught me the Rejang every day after the Baris lesson. Even though the repeating dance cycle was very brief, Kakul insisted that I practice each step very slowly until I was capable of maintaining a "Presence" of effortless grace.

On the night that I was to perform the Rejang, Kakul made the flowers for my headdress and Ibu wrapped me in the many layers of the ceremonial dress. Then the whole family walked to the Pura Desa. Kakul made the proper introductions, so that I would be positioned directly behind the respected old dancer. The *gamelan* played the ancient melody, and the same young women, girls, and toddlers followed in their turns. I completed the crossing with a feeling of deep appreciation for the people who had accepted my offering to their village gods.

The next night, Kakul arranged for a rehearsal with the *gamelan* in Blahbatuh. Kakul intoned the sounds of individual instruments, coordinating the movements with their original impulses. "Each step will have its own sound from the *gamelan*."

Kakul sat next to the drummer and told him to begin, continuing to call out his directions as vocal accompaniment to the *gamelan*.

Comedy interlude

"Feel your feet plant and sink into the ground. If you really feel the spirit of the dance and the sounds, your fingers will shake and tremble. Allow the music to lead you just now; then you will lead it. Listen only to the gongs; blend your movements with the gong and take inspiration from the drum."

Kakul moved in close behind me, forcefully bending my hands into the exact position signaled by the *gamelan*. The large gong resounded; the vibration surged through my body. Kakul insisted that the hands and fingers and toes all listen to the sounds. The total impact of the music had to move through the dancer and be communicated as attitudes of power, complementary in force to the *gamelan*. After the rehearsal we rested, drank *kopi*, watched the practice of the Baris duet, and Kakul spoke of other aspects of competition.

"My students must dance with subtle and strong movements. Refined yet powerful: *halus*. Everything must be precise and dynamic. Then you will surely win! T.'s students have style but no substance, much bravura yet the total effect is that of a fried banana."

Kakul reeled with laughter and then broke into an intensely modulated song from the Arja:

OOOOOOOOOOOOOOOOOO my love pines on
Seeking the beeeeeeloooooved
In an endless quest and YYYYYYYYYlaaaaarning.

His eyes moved coyly to one side, shifted to a distant gaze, and lingered, as if momentarily finding respite from longing. Then they snapped back; his forehead wrinkled and tears seemed to fill his eyes. A shift to sadness, the remembrance of the lover; sweet sadness, the relishing of the memory; strong sadness, a resignation turning to anger. He moved through each distinct and exact feeling with total commitment, agility, and precision: true and stirring.

He broke into laughter and winked. "All expression dwells within you. It must come from inside and pass through you. Do not forget this!"

In the final scenes of the dance-drama, the widow Chalonarang becomes the witch, Rangda

The Warrior exits

The Dalem enters

The Topéng performed at the celebration of the Pura Dalem in Blahbatuh was of exceptional quality. The plot was extensive, full of brilliant dialogue, elaborate character development, battle scenes, resurrections, and invocations of spirits from other realms. But before the performance began, much time was spent sitting on the *balé* behind the stage area discussing the plot with a village priest.

Because the Topéng, as well as other classical dance forms in Bali, do not use a written script, each dancer's role is determined by the priest's directions. After the priest explained the broad outline of the story to Kakul, Kakul assigned the roles to the dancers in his troupe, and then each actor interpreted and developed his roles as he wished. Much of the interpretation depended on knowledge passed along by the priest, and this gave authority to the oral tradition. But ultimately it was the ingenuity, and humor of the Topéng actors themselves that decided whether or not the performance would be received as a successful offering by the villagers as well as by their village gods.

Although the dancers had arrived early in the evening, they did not begin dressing immediately. Kakul had assigned the roles while extensive ceremonies were conducted in the inner temple sanctuaries. Then the five actors engaged in lively conversation, probed arguments related to the story, drank endless rounds of coffee, and smoked *kreteks.* Finally, after midnight, they all agreed on the subtle distinctions of the priest's story. They began to put on their costumes and signaled the other performers, myself included, to prepare their makeup.

The first Baris solo was performed by T.'s student, an eight-year-old boy. I danced next, and after me another of T.'s students performed Jauk. The audience laughed at the Jauk dancer, not because of his humorous interpretation of the playful masked spirit but because his posture was sloppy

Gamelan musicians

instead of compact and strong. He completed his dance nonetheless; but when he removed his mask backstage, he appeared embarrassed. After this solo, one of Kakul's students performed the Topéng Keras, followed by a *tour de force* performance of the Baris duet by the two young girls. They were fearless and aggressive, and danced each step with bravura and control.

T. was absent from the performance, despite an invitation, and this was interpreted as a sign of default in the unofficial competition between his students and Kakul's. Throughout the night, Kakul's students were praised for their spirit as well as their fine classical dance form.

The Topéng drama began immediately after these silent dances and continued at an unrelenting pace for three hours.

The full moon was setting behind the paddies as the chartered *bémo* drove the troupe back to Batuan. The usual barking and harassment by mangy village dogs did not occur. The sound of crickets in the distance became fainter as the cocks began to crow. Kakul had collected his payment of offerings, which had been blessed by a *pedanda* during the night. Back at the family compound, he laid out his bounty in the shrine garden, on the *balé* where the masks were housed. His grandson, Ketut, tended the kerosene lamp at his side. Then, retiring to his porch, he confirmed, with a wink at me, that his victory was secure. The next morning, he did not listen to the gossip that villagers brought to his compound; he only accepted congratulations for his students' performances.

Contemporary Javanese dance

At 7 a.m., I Ketut Rinda arrived in the compound and announced that the regional director of the Indonesian National Dance Academy had appointed him and Kakul to choreograph a new drama. The Academy, created to preserve traditional Indonesian dance and to encourage the choreography of new works based on these traditional forms, was celebrating its tenth anniversary. Pak Rinda said that there was no time to lose, as the event was scheduled to take place in Jogjakarta, Java, in a month's time. He told Kakul that a car from the Academy was waiting for them and that they must leave immediately.

As they walked to the car, Pak Rinda explained to Kakul: "We will create this drama with the utmost respect for Mpu Panuluh, who lived in Kediri, East Java, long ago. He is the author of the famous literary work *Kakawin Hariwangsa*. Our production, Parwa Hariwangsa, takes its story from both the *kakawin* of the Old Javanese *lontar* text and the *parwa* of the Mahabharata. I will prepare a narration of songs and dialogue. We will orchestrate the drama with music from the Wayang Kulit, and you will develop the characters and choreography.

"The story tells of Lord Kresna as the reincarnation of Wisnu, with all the greatness, splendor, and beauty of Dwarawati, the Kingdom of Kresna."

Pak Rinda elaborated the plot in great detail, and by the time the car approached the streamlined concrete structure that had recently replaced the rickety old bridge just outside the city limits of Denpasar, he had completed the first half of the story.

Classical Javanese dance

Arjuna

"... and then Lord Kresna kidnapped his beloved Dewi Sri, who, reincarnated as Dewi Rukmini, was unknowingly betrothed to another."

In the second half of the drama, the consequences of this act were demonstrated in full measure as a battle of horrifying and enormous proportions took place.

"... the battle suddenly lost its mundane meaning. Kresna, who transformed into a manifestation of Wisnu, confronted Arjuna, who also transformed into another manifestation of Wisnu. The implication was that there would never be a resolution to their battle and only the destruction of the world would be possible. ..."

Pak Rinda finished his interpretation of the story just as the car arrived at the National Dance Academy. Kakul and Pak Rinda met with Dr. I Wayan Mertha Sutedja, the director of the Academy. He gathered the members of the production together and delivered a brief speech about the significance of using an excerpt from the shadow puppet theater to symbolize allegiance to their country. Everyone applauded his speech, which stressed the role of the National Dance Academy in upholding the principles of national unity.

Casting began immediately. Obvious selections were completed the first day. The roles of the refined King, Kresna, and his counterpart Arjuna went to two handsome and talented male dancers who had studied the Topéng with Kakul. The role of the Queen, Dewi Rukmini, went to a beautiful delicate-featured woman of royal birth. One of the large good-humored Attendants was cast. And two men who had danced the Baris with great strength were cast in the role of the Barong, one supporting the enormous head and mask, and the other supporting the tail end. Some of the other roles were more difficult, so Kakul and Pak Rinda decided to schedule auditions and work with several dancers at the same time. Then they began to review the melodies with the musicians from Sukawati. The first rehearsal adjourned before sunset. All the musicians piled into the back of a small *bémo* for the trip home and got out at Sukawati; Kakul, who was sitting in the cab with Pak Rinda, got out at the crossroads in Batuan after arranging to meet the *bémo* there the next day.

The playful Barong, prelude to Parwa Hariwangsa

Lord Kresna and Dewi Rukmini

Rangda stalks the Barong

Every day throughout the following weeks, Kakul went to Denpasar. Act by act, he developed the choreography of the play. As he choreographed for each dancer or group of dancers, Pak Rinda followed behind him, singing poetry and speaking the dialogue that accompanied the dance. In this way the dancers, sandwiched between Kakul and Pak Rinda, were able to learn voice and dance simultaneously. At first, many of them experienced difficulty with this method of instruction, but Kakul gently coaxed them with his humor. Kakul emphasized the precision of classical postures and gestures from Pak Rinda's dance *lontars*. It was a welcome challenge for the fine dancers of the Academy.

Ketut Rinda sang in old Javanese verse:

Act One
In the Kingdom of Kundina wherein
Kesari the Queen's Attendant enters and tells of the
Happiness of her heart on the morning of the wedding
Everything is ready in the Reception Hall for her mistress Dewi
Rukmini.

Kakul swaggered around the great hall of the Academy, sashaying and playfully swinging his behind. He stopped and faced the stage entrance, putting his hands into a gesture of respect. The agile dancer followed his steps, arriving just behind him. Kakul turned and showed her the position of the fingers.

"If you address Her Highness Dewi Rukmini, you must demonstrate the proper respect allotted to one of such high rank. You will bend at the waist and attend to each word, making sure not to offend the Queen with low manners or by losing attention. You will do this throughout your conversations. When you are not in the presence of the Queen, your character is one of a fun-loving, jovial spirit, and you are free to cavort and play. But now, before the Queen appears, you will assume this posture."

Kakul left Kesari and rushed to the center stage entrance, through which the Queen was preparing to enter. Ketut Rinda continued singing as Kakul posed in front of the Queen, indicating a posture of gentleness and authority:

Dewi Rukmini enters from the inner palace and tells of the
Sadness of her heart as
She is to be married to one she does not love.

Kakul spoke as he demonstrated the Queen's dance: "You will walk slowly, almost imperceptibly; your heavenly presence is a gift to this mundane world, and your attitudes must be conveyed by every lingering expression or tone in your voice. You are beyond time, and there exists no effort in your entire being."

Ketut Rinda elaborated:

Dewi Rukmini possesses a firm will and
Expresses her desire that Lord Kresna will be her true husband
She waits in the garden for his arrival later that evening.

Kesari called all the Royal Attendants to accompany the Queen to the garden. Six angelic dancers formed a circle around the Queen, with Kesari leading them. Kakul demonstrated the movements necessary to create the illusion of a boat about to embark on a journey.

"All together you will guide the vessel that carries the Queen." He ran in front of the group, leading them like waves on the open sea, in rhythmic, cresting movements. They knelt as the Queen entered and performed a solo dance, displaying her grace and charm. Kakul led her every step, insisting that she bend her knees more and lift up at the shoulders. He shifted to the character of Kesari, demonstrating a swaggering walk around the Royal Attendants. Leaving her in mid-circle, he returned to the Attendants, who eased the departure of the entire entourage, and ended the first act.

I Ketut Rinda

The next day Ketut Rinda called out again, announcing the beginning of the rehearsal:

Act Two
In the Kingdom of Kundina
In another part of the palace, wherein
Delem and Sangut the jovial servants enter and
Talk about their happiness.

Kakul choreographed these characters in the ridiculous masks of the Topéng. But during rehearsals the masks were used only for inspiration, and the characters were built on movement and facial expressions alone. Kakul yanked on Sangut's tail.

"You! You are stupid. But somehow you've managed to develop a sense of humor and have become a major irritation to Delem, who takes himself altogether too seriously. But since he's your superior, you must respect him by displaying the usual courtesies accorded to rank. There's no one lower than you. Kresna's Attendant, Merdah, is your equal but by the time you meet him, there will have been a terrific battle. Until then, you can tease Delem, but you mustn't cross him, because he is responsible for your safekeeping."

Ketut Rinda continued chanting, following the choreography, instructing the actors in modulations of voice and pitch.

Lord Sisupala enters and everyone shares his happiness
Tomorrow he will be married with Dewi Rukmini.
The Kings and all the Guests have already arrived
They will witness and give prayer and blessings for the ceremony.

During the next three days, Kakul marked out the scene of the kidnap; a love dance between Kresna and Dewi Rukmini; the outraged Sisupala enlisting the assistance of the mighty Pandawas; a scene of deceit; and a confrontation between two Ghastly Angry Kings. He further choreographed the roles of the refined Kresna and his jovial Attendants, of several Righteous Kings, and of the Head and Tail of the playful protecting Barong and his Monkey friend. With each change in role, Kakul revealed his expertise in transformation, never stopping long enough to allow the characterization to fade, yet always making a clean and distinct break, as if he had just changed a mask. No expression was duplicated; each attitude, gesture, and emotional nuance was unique to its own role.

Ketut Rinda announced a battle scene: Kakul and his son Kantor enacted the rapid, calculating combat, first between Bhima and King Baladewa, then between the two refined Kings, Arjuna and Kresna. Now the movements became a study in fluid combat, alluding to the magical powers that both opponents possessed. Kakul struck a delicate pose, extending one hand in a sacred gesture; the other, securing the dagger that would be used in the battle, was poised on his hip. He advanced slowly, not revealing the weapon until the moment before the strike. Then, with lightning precision, his head tucked into his chest, he extended one hand forward to immobilize his opponent and with the other hand delivered the deadly blow.

Kakul rehearsing Parwa

Kakul choreographing the battle scene

Kakul assumed the posture of one, then a second Rangda. As the two aspects of Wisnu in opposition, evoking terror in a vortex of mire, the Rangdas stalked in circles.

Ketut Rinda sang out in conclusion:

Lord Yudistira and the gods requested mercy from Wisnu
So that the world would not be destroyed
And further requested that all those who had fallen in battle
Be brought back to life.

By the end of the first week of rehearsals, Kakul was fully absorbed in the production of the Parwa. He had choreographed all the main characters, and the minor characters were in sketch form. Rehearsals now lasted into the night, sometimes well past midnight.

On his first day's rest, Kakul was at work in the rice paddies by 5 a.m. He returned to the compound two hours later, assembled the shell headdresses for about an hour, reviewed the Baris with me, and gave a lesson to the two young girls from Blahbatuh.

That night Kakul, his nephew, and I sat on the *balé* in the family compound. Kakul told of a dream in which he flew over the ocean. He was not certain of the implications of this act, but confided several possibilities.

"Certain precautions are necessary before discussing such deep feelings. Your thoughts must be focused and contained, so that you do not become open to the powers of black magic."

He whispered that there was a *warung* next to the Pura Desa in Batuan whose proprietor was rumored to practice black magic.

"If you spend much time gossiping near this stand, the proprietor will come to know your fears and desires. He makes use of idle talk and jokes to gain the confidence of insecure souls."

The family huddled around a kerosene lamp sharing tales of ghosts, visions, and possessions. On the opposite porch, Kantor's wife, Chirī, threw the wooden shuttle across her loom; the only other sound was a cowbell clanking gently. All else was silent.

Most of the work on the production of the Parwa was completed as Galungan approached. The director of the Academy had already praised the choreography, and during the rehearsals Kakul perfected the continuity between scenes and refined dance gestures. Pak Rinda devoted much of his time to correcting nuances of dialogue and song.

On the evening before Galungan, Kakul's grandchildren placed offerings at the usual spots in the family compound, places they favored spontaneously and places required by custom: in the shrine garden, at the entrance to the compound, at the four cardinal points of the joining walls around the compound, and at the crossroads. A few grains of white rice were placed on a sliver of banana leaf and put on the ground. Dogs followed the children on their route and ate the offerings. For a week Chirī and Ibu had been making fantastic offerings—whorls, spirals, and pendants. Now they worked long into the night assembling the intricately sculpted palm leaves.

Later, in the black of the night, villagers slaughtered scores of huge, succulent pigs for traditional bloodletting sacrifice. Torrents of rain muffled the sounds of shrieking animals, and by the time the sun came up, on a crystalline day, the smell of suckling pigs, roasting on six-foot skewers, filled the air.

The Gunung Agung rose above a halo of clouds, as if clearing a path for the gods. The paddies were empty; all the villagers were busy with preparation of food and receiving guests. A plethora of offerings filled every path in the *banjar:* flowers placed on the ground in woven palm baskets; coconut husks, quartered and charred with incense. The *penjors*—each one topped by a dangling ornament that gently pulled it into an arc—created a series of interconnecting tunnels over the village lanes. They swayed in the hot fragrant winds. The offerings and devotional objects, assembled in contemplation of the Godhead, Sang Hyang Widhi, were strewn about; they were placed on tiny platforms in front of the family com-

Kakul giving last-minute instructions to Bima

The attendants

pounds; they lined the paths throughout the village and floated in the irrigation canals. The scene repeated itself everywhere—awaiting the gods to descend and inhabit shrines all over the island.

In Kakul's garden the shrines were open. Each revealed a sacred treasure: ancestral possessions, amulets, tokens with white magic inscriptions, or palm weavings in the form of Dewi Sri.

Gongs and drums resounded just outside the compound. A friendly Barong strolled in the morning sun accompanied by a throng of children and a small portable *gamelan*. The children pulled on the Barong's tail, which was decorated with bells; and the creature taunted and teased them in return by shaking its great mane, bringing its Protecting Spirit to each household in the *banjar*.

When the young Baris dancers from Blahbatuh arrived, Kakul invited everyone into the shrine garden. He announced that he had been asked to perform the sacred Topéng solo on Kuningan, the end of the ten-day New Year celebration, closing the ceremony with a performance of Sidha Karya.

"The Sidha Karya is the last, and the most difficult, of all masks to perform. But without him, the Topéng Pajegan cannot be successfully completed. I must make special offerings of rice from the temple of Sidha Karya, located in the south, very far from here, and must prepare myself in deep contemplation before the performance.

Villagers watch as Rangda prepares for the final transformation

Pendet, an offering dance

"If the soul is not completely pure," Kakul went on, "there's danger in performing many transformations. But if I connect with the *taksu*, I will be strong enough to allow many spirits to pass through my body without allowing them to become lodged or blighted on my soul. I must make offerings that will purify me. Then the *taksu* will enter and guide my movements. I know when the *taksu* has entered and the audience knows it as well.

"Then if I perform with ten masks, I will have the purity of soul necessary to move beyond the realms of my body's strength. If I perform with fifteen masks, I will have the intention to receive powers beyond my control. And if I dance with twenty masks, I will be as open to the source of consciousness as a lotus in its unfolding. But still, my sacred duty is incomplete without the Sidha Karya."

Kakul told the two young girls that they would precede

Bumblebee dance

the Topéng Pajegan, and informed me that I would open the performance with the Baris solo. "Incidentally," he added, "I assume that your dancing will be perfect."

For the next nine days, Kakul's activities expanded beyond what seemed possible for one person to accomplish. In the mornings he instructed the young girls in the development of more varied expression during their interactions.

"Your combat is not merely an act of aggression. You must display pride. You must be able to intimidate your opponent with the slightest glance. During a victory stance, it's not sufficient to gloat; this must also be a time to contemplate and reconsider your position. Turn these moments to thoughts from within. It is in these moments that a trust with the audience is established. In this way you will gain their respect and never lose their support."

After the duet instructions, my own lessons now focused on the intensification of strength.

"When you open the curtain, you must be prepared to fight! In this moment, all is decided about your power. This pose is the one with the most tension, yet it must convey total control and poise."

After the lessons, Kakul left the village for rehearsals at the Academy in Denpasar. The final stage of production was in progress, and the performers usually played the entire drama several times through each day.

Kakul came back from rehearsals very tired, his thoughts filled with the dimensions of the Parwa choreography, the approaching tour of Java, getting his workers together to plow in the paddies at dawn, and, finally, the sacraments for the Topéng Pajegan—not to mention his inner preparations for this intense performance.

"The masks will be seen as symbols of the ancestors," he explained, "and it is my sacred duty to receive their magic, to allow it to enter me and animate the masks, one after the other, until I am exhausted. After the performance, I must make the proper offerings to ensure the release of this magic from my being, to ensure its return to the realms unknown to us, and to ensure the departure of any evil spirits who have witnessed the performance. And my offering must be great enough to provide for the return of the *taksu* on the next occasion of the sacred performance. This is of absolute importance. This is the essence of the offering, as it is the gesture of thanking the gods. The sacred words bind us to our ancestors, to their revelations—to their very existence."

The night before the Topéng Pajegan, I was sitting alone on my porch. It was after midnight and the kerosene in the lamp burned very low. I contemplated that morning's exhausting lesson. The transition from the first part of the dance, the "wild part," to the second part, a slow agile walk, had been complex, accomplished with the beat of the drum. The totality of the change was elusive to me, the slow steps awkward, my inclination to bolt unsuitable. Deliberateness was inappropriate for this venture into another aspect of the Warrior. Kakul had played the music for the new movement so slowly that my awkwardness was even more apparent.

"If you slow the movement until it is barely visible, the power becomes more dynamic. It can be distilled and transformed, then reconstructed."

The already difficult eye movements were further complicated by rapid darting to each side after every third step. Occasionally, my concentration lapsed into utter confusion and Kakul insisted that we begin over again. Kakul imitated the instruments to give the cues for each move. He continued in this manner for several hours. He ignored frustration and fatigue and went on playing the melody.

"Again," he said without looking up. Then in the middle of a step he yelled, "Bend elbows!" Or, "Eyes not fierce enough!" Or, "Lips like this!" and he mimed sweet, subtle smiles.

"Kantor will give you a lesson again this afternoon, and my son Rějug will be here to criticize and perfect your dance. Rějug has stature. Listen to his suggestions and watch how agile an enormous dancer who has grace can be."

The lesson ended when Kakul's grandson came running into the shrine garden to announce that the car from the Dance Academy was waiting for him at the crossroads. Kakul left in the middle of a step and went off to bathe. I collapsed into a chair and drank the cold coffee that Ibu had prepared at the beginning of the lesson. Kakul reappeared several minutes later looking very cosmopolitan in his olive-green Levi pants and white Oxford shirt. He wore city sandals and wrapped a wool sweater around his shoulders as he waved goodbye, yelling, *"Ciao!"* Since rehearsals continued to be exceedingly long, I assumed that I wouldn't see him until the next day.

During the late afternoon lesson, with Rějug observing, Kantor placed the shell crown on my head. "Try now to get a feel for the crown," he said. "The intensity of the movement causes different sounds. Find a threshold for the tinkling of the delicate shells. Think of it as an expression of inner dynamic tension."

After rehearsing several times, the day was gone and I felt my strength begin to ebb. I went into my room to rest, and dozed off.

Through the window, Kakul's voice awakened me gently: "Get up, get up." I stumbled out of bed and, half asleep, went out onto the porch. I hardly remembered having fallen asleep; my clothes were rumpled. The lamp on the porch was dim now; Kakul's face was barely visible. The glow highlighted his eyes and his smile. He giggled softly. I focused my eyes on his face: his forehead was smooth and high; his eyes, surrounded by lines, gleamed and danced in quiet excitement. He raised one eyebrow and mimicked the eye movements from the Baris.

Topéng Pajegan

His voice was low as he told me about the rehearsals. "The character of Bhima is very difficult. I must resolve to find in his movement a tender yet large, exaggerated expression.

"Of course, the source for the characters—their gestures, and attitudes—are all to be found in Ketut Rinda's *lontars,* and he is an expert in such interpretation. Other characters and movements I myself have distilled from the Gambúh: I've drawn inspiration for Arjuna from Panji, Hero, Warrior, Artist, Lover, Scholar—constantly changing identities, recounting histories of ancient kingdoms, philosophy and religion, resolving battles and encountering romance. And the movements themselves: for instance, the wavelike rowing gestures of the Queen's Attendants are, in fact, called the 'rowing of a boat' in the Gambúh. Then a slight tilt of the head, called *nyingak bebek,* ends the rowing movement. *Bebek,* a little duck, checks the situation in a subtle way, as if a falcon were lurking over the prey. The duck does not turn its head toward the attacker to reveal awareness. It only looks up with its eyes, bravely but with caution. Then it checks back to its ducklings, just in case an attack does occur.

"Other movements I've taken directly from nature. As with the playful Monkey who is the Barong's friend. One day, I was walking through the Monkey Forest and I noticed a monkey kneeling by a stream. I decided to stay for several days in the forest with this monkey to learn its ways, its "voice," its days and nights, the way in which it extended an arm, relaxed or attacking. Sad eyes and monkey sounds, monkey scratch; a sudden lunge-shift in stance. Check the situation again: all's clear! Grab the fruit! Then shift back onto haunches to enjoy the meal."

Kakul laughed with utter abandon, rolling in his chair as a Monkey King would.

He was silent again. His attention went to the other side of the courtyard. It was dark there, with no activity except the occasional scratching of the fighting cocks. He became serious. All expression and animation left his face as he got up and walked to the cages where the cocks were kept. I heard some rustling and then there was a faint muttering. Kakul came back to the porch holding his pet fighting cock under one arm, stroking it with his other hand. He sat down and continued to stroke it. The animal gurgled and responded with feisty wing-flapping. Kakul bounced it gently on his knees and the cock was still.

"Kings have not seen what I have seen," he said in a low voice. "They have not been on the trains in America, or worn tweed coats, bowler hats, and black leather shoes in London. They have not pranced through modern hotel lobbies while pedestrians paused in amazement.

"They have not walked down Wilshire Boulevard in Los Angeles, into the most exclusive jewelry stores, and dared to bargain with the proprietors."

He threw his head back and laughed and laughed and laughed.

"You see this?" He raised one hand to form a *mudra* and extended his neck, his head bobbing back and forth as if it were on a pivot. Kakul danced with his face, ferocious as the fighting cock on his lap. The *mudra* extended his being into another realm.

"This is my jet."

In an instant he flicked the gesture to the night and his hand swooped down: "JJJJet!"

His eyes flashed, darting back and forth. He laughed softly.

"No jet. No money can buy this, you know."

He extended and raised both arms, as if leaving the earth; the *mudra* propelled him with the force of his soul.

"The dance," he said quietly. "The movement; this is my jet."

Fluttering white clouds turn to cream yellow, turn to orange, turn to red. Stillness and only the sound of water rushing out of a coconut shell spout.

Sunset on the rice fields.

The rice forever there, each *sawah* flooded in growth or harvest. A white stork wings its way home. Palm branches like statues; the sky's too-brilliant color disappears behind shimmering gray dusk.

Four women sitting on the paddy edge, resting, smoking.

Listen to the *gamelan*! A flute gently rows the boat across the expanse of heaven. Four women journey in the mist. Slowly crossing an endless ocean of rice. Waves in the paddies. The Queen rises in a haze. Fiery red crowns the palms, and currents stir the first darkness of night. . .

The Topéng is about to begin. Kakul stands next to the box containing his masks.

Om, Grandfather, Great God,
Om, Grandmother, Great God,
Please wake up, come forth, and act.

Kakul strikes the box three times. *"Pomo, pomo, pomo."*

Then quickly, as soon as the Spirit has entered into him, he opens the box and puts on the first mask.

Later, calm, the performance complete, Kakul closes the mask box:

Hail, Grandfather, Great God,
Hail, Grandmother, Great God,
Return now,
Be in the Holy Place, each one.
Hail the Name, Om.

SHIFTING TIME

Four years later, I returned to Bali. The *bémo* fare to the capital city of Denpasar had increased 400 percent, and I had to tranfer to another vehicle inside the city to go to Peliatan.

I went to the main marketplace to buy coffee and Ovaltine before departing on the local *bémo*. Having found a seat in a *warung* across the street from the main bus station, I was able to wait for a streamlined Colt Wagon while I watched the hubbub in the market.

People descended stairs leading into an enormous cavern. Stall vendors sold herbs, spices, cloth, and other local commodities such as tobacco and sweet cakes. At the bottom of the stairs, the aisle disappeared behind the food vendors and then came into the clearing in front of the woven basket goods and then wound through the section of the market that sold only pungent roots and an inconceivable number of aromatic condiments. A spectrum of faces passed by. Blurs became distinct: an old Chinese woman, her white hair tied in a bun, wearing an intricately detailed Javanese batik sarong and a lace *kebaya* fastened tight at the bosom with gold safety pins connected to each other on a small gold chain.

Balinese women merchants passed by with wares piled high on their heads; they mingled with Indian textile merchants, Chinese dry-goods vendors, and Javanese entrepreneurs. A few stalls were tended by men wearing pajamas and white T-shirts. Mobile *warungs* swung by on the shoulders of agile young peddlers searching for suitable morning business locations, which would be abandoned as the peak hours passed.

Children darted in and out of sight. Some of them were shrewd in the ways of money and hustling, always looking for a load to carry for a rich shopkeeper or tourist. Many of the children, orphaned during the coup of 1965, had organized themselves into groups and become proficient in bartering. They knew how to get the best prices and their skills were sought out by overworked servants.

Adults in slinky jeans and skinny French motto-emblazoned shirts paraded on the main boulevard. "Rive Gauche" walked by sporting an immaculately coiffed shag and platform shoes. He carried an Italian briefcase, a symbol of his high status in the burgeoning local economy.

Kites circled the distant sky; the heat and dust of the day turned to the intense reds of sunset and mixed with a constantly changing landscape of people.

Finally the *bémo*, loaded with passengers, departed for Peliatan. In the south of the island electricity reached into the *banjar* of every village connected to the main route. The money-taker said that in some villages television was available as far back as three kilometers from the terminal located on the thoroughfare. Rice fields laced with poles and wires slashed the view of the Gunung Agung. The conveniences provided by technology illuminated some of the tangent lanes with glaring fluorescent tubes, and an occasional small *warung* had forsaken the kerosene lantern for the light bulb.

At a *warung* in Peliatan, the owner's son proudly announced that he was going to the *balé banjar* to watch the nightly TV broadcast, consisting of *News from Djakarta and the World* and *I Love Lucy*.

"He enjoys watching the beast," his mother teased, and the teenager went away noticeably embarrassed.

"This TV is a terrible demon. As far as I'm concerned, it has made him ill." The Ibu made motions as if wiping her brow back and forth, and had a pained expression on her face.

"He's become confused. He's distracted and lazy. *Aduuh,* he has no concentration anymore. Sometimes, when I talk to him, I think that he's in a daze."

A friend of Ketut's entered the *warung*. He had just returned from making offerings in the courtyard of a Brahmana family that was performing the soul-raising ceremonies preceding a relative's cremation.

"I don't know," he said, shaking his head. "This policy of family planning is really not mentioned in the *lontars*. It certainly makes new interpretation of the sacred texts very complex. Maybe these new policies will make it difficult, or even impossible, for a soul to reincarnate in the known paths. In the past, we liked to give our ancestors ample opportunity to return. We had very large families, maybe eight or ten children. . . . Even the release of the soul has been affected. Now

that we have electricity in the *banjar* and on the main road, we must limit the height of the cremation tower. Of course, we disconnect all the power on the day of the cremation, but this sort of cooperation only connects us with the official worldly hierarchy. The true authority of the gods is in jeopardy. A soul seeking to aspire to heaven through a many-layered tower will now have to confront powerful obstacles."

The following morning, I went to the village of Batuan. At the *warung* next to the crossroads, two farmers were discussing the change in rice cultivation.

"There's already organized opposition to using new hybrid rice strains. The new rice is short, squat, and ugly, unlike the elegant stalks of our ancient strains. Most of this so-called improved rice has to be harvested and removed from the stalks in the fields, to be sold directly from the *sawahs*. No stored crops—we've lost our savings accounts! And when we bring the few bundles to the granaries, it molds and rats eat it. Foreign rice doesn't hold a shape when fashioned into offering cakes. All we have is cash; then we must buy fine Balinese rice in the stores!"

"*Béh!*" responded his friend.

"New chemicals have only brought havoc to our fields, not to mention what's happening to our village funds. One year, the fertilizers produce a four-crop harvest, and the next year, the soil is dead, burned and depleted of all natural fertilizers.

"We must maintain control of our fields; leaf compost, ash, and animal manures are the best. Dependence on foreign merchants for chemical fertilizers and pesticides is destroying the stability of our local economy."

He continued, detailing the changes that affected his daily life. "And to make things even worse, the rice mills take all the vitamins out of our superb rice and turn it into waste: the husks of the kernels, removed by the heat generated in the huge machines, becomes pig feed. The pigs are fat and the people are sick. Now we are advised to buy vitamins in a bottle to supplement our deficient diets."

"*Béh*, this makes you crazy," concluded his comrade.

The first farmer continued: "In my *banjar*, we still pound the rice with bamboo poles. We enjoy our work because we like to make the body strong. I still climb coconut trees to make palm wine."

He paused, relishing the pride of a man in his late sixties whose body is limber and relaxed. "I am fit; I cut rice and this gives me life. But my sons don't work in the paddies. Soon fewer people will be needed to work in the fields, and our local economy, and our lives, will change even more radically."

I resumed my dance studies, but now with Kakul's son Kantor. Kakul had suffered a stroke. His right leg was paralyzed and he could not speak. But when I practiced the Topéng Dalem, he eloquently demonstrated the gestures that I had performed incorrectly. The old master was still able to express more with one hand in a few minutes than most performers are capable of expressing in an entire performance. He remained unrivaled; his gestures still exuded the power of a burning heart, whose fire refused to be extinguished.

THE LION AND THE BULL

Once there were two Bagawans; the elder was called Wasipta and the younger was called Sri Aji Darma Swami. They lived in the district of Kediri, not far from each other. The Holy Man Wasipta was a herder of cows and Sri Aji Darma Swami sold firewood.

The cows that Bagawan Wasipta tended belonged to the God Weraspati, who was the father of Siwa. The bull was named Sang Nandaka and he was hairy, black, and very soft. The female was called Sang Nandini and she was hairy, white, and very soft.

One day, Wasipta, very sad because the life of a cow herder is very difficult, without much compensation for work, went to the small temple that belonged to his employer, and during his meditations, he told the God Weraspati of his woes.

The God Weraspati answered him immediately: "Looking after the two cows is your job; therefore you must do your job well. From today onward, you may sell the milk of Sang Nandini but only for use during certain important ceremonies."

This response greatly reassured Wasipta, and he offered his thanks to Weraspati.

From then on, many people came to the Holy Man to buy milk for their important ceremonies, and Wasipta became quite wealthy. He repaired his house, and built a temple to worship the god, and he was always able to make large offerings.

One day while the Holy Man Wasipta was meditating in his temple, his brother Sri Aji Darma Swami visited him. He had heard about Wasipta's good fortune.

Wasipta asked his brother to sit down and said to him, "Allow me to continue my meditation and I will be with you momentarily."

After he had finished his meditation, he turned to his young brother and said, "How are you doing? Maybe you have already heard of my good fortune? My life is very different now, thank God. And now don't be bashful. Please, ask for what you want and I will give it to you."

Sri Aji Darma Swami replied, "Thank you very much for offering such generosity to me. Of course I came here to ask you for something. I'd like you to give me Sang Nandaka, your bull."

His brother was startled.

"The cows were a present from the God Weraspati, but since I have already extended my generosity toward you, I will give you the bull. But only on one condition: Sang Nandaka is a sign of Grace. Look after him well and do not work him hard."

Sri Aji Darma Swami agreed and took Sang Nandaka to his dwelling.

Sri Aji Darma Swami broke his promise immediately and began working Sang Nandaka very hard collecting firewood. Very soon, Sri Aji Darma Swami became a rich man and, within a short time, owned 120 cows besides Sang Nandaka.

One day, Sri Aji Darma Swami wished to go to the big market in Madura and take with him enormous loads of firewood to sell. He loaded up all 120 cows with packs of wood and on Sang Nandaka he placed an extra-heavy load.

Sang Nandaka thought: Béh, this load is too heavy. I'll fool Sri Aji Darma Swami by pretending to fall. He cares more about his wealth than about kindness. I'm really very angry at him.

After the caravan had journeyed down the road a short distance, Sang Nandaka fell. His driver, Si Cokot, ran to Sri Aji Darma Swami to tell him: "I ask for your pardon, sir, but Sang Nandaka has fallen under his heavy load!"

They both ran to the spot where the bull lay fallen, and Sri Aji Darma Swami said, "How can you cause me such shame by falling? All you want to do is eat. Truly you have fallen because you are lazy. Si Cokot, you must leave Sang Nandaka right here on this spot. Kill him and bury him."

Now Si Cokot thought in his heart: Why must I kill Sang Nandaka? I'll just lead him to the Great Forest and turn him loose, but I'll tell Sri Aji Darma Swami that I slaughtered the bull.

He then spoke out loud: "Sang Nandaka, I implore you to wake up."

The bull jumped to his feet, and Si Cokot said: "I'll take you to the Great Forest and tell Sri Aji Darma Swami that you've been slaughtered."

Sang Nandaka thanked him, and then Si Cokot returned to the caravan.

Now, Sang Nandaka was free to live in the Great Forest and could eat anything he wanted.

The King of the Forest was the Mighty Lion, Raja Singha, and he lived on top of Mount Melawa. Raja Singha had four dogs who served as his Ministers: Semade, who was the eldest; I Nohan; I Tatit; and I Kanchil.

One day, the King asked his Ministers to see if there were any new animals disturbing his Kingdom, for he did not want to be challenged. When the Ministers arrived in the Great Forest, they were very surprised to encounter Sang Nandaka.

The Ministers called to him, "Hey, Big Animal, what are you doing here? What's your name and where do you come from? And why are you eating everything in sight? You haven't even asked for permission from our King. When we tell the King about you, he'll probably want to kill you."

Sang Nandaka roared with laughter and answered, "Why do you want to know about me? No matter; my name is Sang Nandaka and I'm not afraid of your King. It's all right for me to eat in the Forest and I certainly don't need to ask permission from anyone. If he wants to fight with me, then I'll fight!"

The Ministers ran back to Raja Singha on top of the Mount, and breathlessly reported: "We beg your pardon, O Raja Singha, but there is a Big Animal, a Bull named Sang Nandaka. We told him that this is your Forest and that you are the King, but he did not believe us. We forbade him to eat anything, but he ignored us. He has no respect for you, Your Highness."

Raja Singha pondered this report and answered, "Well, my Ministers, your report may be true, but since I am a King it is not right for me to be quick to anger. We must simply advise this Bull to leave our Forest and then, if he challenges us, we will be forced to kill him. Do you understand?"

The Ministers answered, "Yes, we understand." And they re-

turned to the Forest to give Sang Nandaka the warning.

As they traveled to meet the Bull, the Eldest Minister, Semade, confided to his comrades: "Raja Singha and Sang Nandaka are both Big Strong Animals. Our King has sharp nails and teeth, and the Bull has sharp horns. If they fight, they'll surely kill each other, and if they kill each other, we'll be the Rulers of this Kingdom."

His three conspirators agreed.

"When we speak with Sang Nandaka, we'll reverse the intention of Raja Singha's message and lure Sang Nandaka into a battle."

After agreeing to this scheme, the Ministers arrived at the place where the Bull was eating.

Semade said to him, "Why are you still here, Sang Nandaka? My King says that you're a Scoundrel and that everything you eat belongs to him. Leave here immediately!"

Sang Nandaka turned to them and answered, "I don't care what your King says. Where is he, anyway? If he wants to fight, I'm not afraid of him. Besides, what reason does he have for forbid-

ding me to eat here? Please tell your King that if he sends me away from here, it is he who is the Scoundrel!"

The Four Ministers ran back to Raja Singha and reported: "Our Lord King, we have just come from talking with Sang Nandaka, and we have delivered your message patiently and slowly. But he immediately challenged us and called you a Scoundrel and challenged you to battle."

After hearing his Ministers, the Lion King charged into the Great Forest and did not stop until he had come upon Sang Nandaka. His Ministers followed behind him, chuckling to themselves.

As soon as Raja Singha saw the Bull, he pounced on him, biting his neck and tearing at his flesh. Sang Nandaka reared, then lunged, piercing the heart of the Raja Singha with his horns. Within a few moments, they both lay bloody and dead.

The Four Ministers, assured that they would have enough Bull and Lion to eat for months, snickered at the success of their plot, and returned to the Mount to rule the Kingdom as they saw fit.

GLOSSARY

aduh	exclamation of surprise.
agung	great.
Aji Pajenengan	Revered Ancestor.
anak	child.
Anak Agung	title used by male members of Satrya caste.
arak	distilled rice wine.
Arja	a folk opera, one of the most popular dramatic forms, which utilizes sung dialogue. Stories come from many sources (Hindu, Arabic, Chinese, Balinese) and usually contain much melodrama and romance. Arja developed out of Gambúh in 1880, with an all-male cast, although today women play the female roles.
Bagawan	title of king who has renounced his earthly possessions to become a holy man.
bagus	good.
balé	a pavilion; a platform bed, or elevated area.
Bali Aga	*see* Gunung Agung.
banjar	district within a village, consisting of a limited number of families whose relationship may be familial and is more usually based on political-geographical structure.
Baris	ancient warrior's drill-dance; from *bebarisan*, literally, a line or row, referring to the line formations of ancient Balinese armies. Over thirty varieties of Baries are extant today, ranging from the ceremonial dances performed by large groups of men with weapons to the more popular, and now secular, Baris, a solo dance form that requires great skill and dexterity.
Barong	mythical beast, protector of the village, spiritual symbol of right livelihood. Dates back to pre-Hindu times. There are many Barongs; most common is Barong Kekek, a dragon creature whose mask embodies the features of a lion, tiger, cow, and goat. Barong Landung, giant male and female puppets, are ''danced'' in village exorcism rituals.
Bhatara	title ascribed to a god.
batik	a cloth made in Java that has been dyed by a wax-resistant method; worn around the lower body.
bebek	a little duck.
béh	exclamation of mild (or substantial) shock.
bémo	a privately owned vehicle used for public transportation; usually a remodeled Datsun pickup truck with facing seat benches on an enclosed rear deck.
Bima	One of the five Pandawas. *See* Pandawas.
bintang baru	new star; Bintang Baru, name of beer sold in Indonesia.
brem	rice wine.
Chalonarang	name of a widow from a twelfth-century kingdom who turned to black magic for revengeful power. Also name of a dance-drama of ritual exorcism which chronicles the story of Chalonarang, or Rangda (literally, widow), who is the manifestation of the Queen of Evil Spirits.
Cili	fertility goddess.
dalang	puppeteer in shadow-theater *(wayang)* tradition; mystic scholar who, while manipulating the puppets of the Wayang Kulit, recounts the ancient lore.

dalem	literally, inside, "within or inner"; metaphysical concept with innumerable aspects and faces. In Topéng, Dalem is the main character, playing the role of virtuous king. The Pura Dalem, commonly translated as Temple of Death, is dedicated to Durga, Goddess of Death, but also to Dewi Sri. The Pura Dalem is always situated on the village outskirts next to the graveyard and the rice fields.
desa	a village; an independent community.
Dewi Sri	goddess of rice and fruits of the earth; masculine: Dewa.
dharma	the way, "life as it is"; Sanskrit word, originally an Indian concept, brought to Indonesia with traditions of Indian religious beliefs. Attribute of people who strive to lead the Noble Life.
Eka Dasa Rudra	a once-in-every-hundred-years celebration.
gado-gado	mixed green vegetables, slightly cooked, smothered with hot spicy peanut sauce.
galak	wild.
Galungan	Balinese New Year lasting ten days; occurs every 210 days.
Gambúh	literally, "way or life of a king"; a dance-drama considered by the Balinese to be the oldest form of classical dance. Court theater performed without masks. Most of the dramatized stories come from the Malat cycle, a collection of tales centered around Panji, a princely figure similar to Arjuna. Because the characters must speak in Kawi, Gambúh is deemed the most difficult of all dance forms to learn.
gamelan	generic name for orchestras and music; usually of bronze gongs, metallophones, bamboo flutes, drums, and so on.
gangsa	metallophone with bronze keys over bamboo-tube resonators.
Gedé	Great; eldest son.
Gunung Agung	volcanic mountain in the east central part of the island of Bali; is symbolic of the Highest Unity.
halus	polished, smooth, refined, perfect. Of utmost concern to all Balinese in content and form. Opposed to *kasar* (crass), which is most undesirable.
Ibu	Indonesian term of respect for married woman; (often used in direct address).
ikat	method of binding groups of threads (usually the warp) with string or bamboo slivers into a design. The bound strands are then dyed and woven; ancient technique of iconography.
Indra	god of the rain and thunder.
jaja	cookies.
Jauk	solo pantomime mask dance of a demonic character.
Jero	literally, inner (corresponds to dalem); title for a low-caste woman who has married a higher-caste man; also polite for "you," used by strangers.
Joged Bungbung	a flirtatious dance performed by young women.
kain	cloth; usually refers to fabric that is wrapped around the lower half of a woman's body; also may refer to specific textiles used in sacred ceremony, such as *kain gringsing*.
kakawin	poetry of the Old Javanese period (ninth to fifteenth century) sung in Bali today in various religious rites.
kakul	snail.
Kawi	poetic language, including Old and Middle Javanese. Since ancient times, the Balinese have maintained several distinct traditions of language (that is, Sanskrit, used mostly by priests; Balinese, literary and vernacular, including several sets of vocabulary determined by social etiquette and caste; and Indonesian, for schools, government, the media, and com-

merce). In theatrical dialogue, one performer speaks or sings the Kawi, or the literary Balinese; the second type of Balinese provides phrase-by-phrase immediate paraphrase into the vernacular, often with extensive commentary. Paraphrasing is the duty of the Penesar in Topéng and probably has always existed in Bali for the simultaneous use of different languages.

kebaya a blouse worn by women; introduced into wide use in Indonesia during the period of Dutch colonization.

kedis kelepuk Balinese dance term: head bobble.

Ketchak a form of chanting, originally used to accompany certain trance dances; today known as the monkey dance, performed only for tourists.

Ketut fourth-born; children of Wesia-caste and Sudra families receive both individual names and names signifying the order of birth: Wayan, firstborn; Madé, second; Nyoman, third; Ketut, fourth. The order is repeated with Wayan, fifth-born, and so on. Hence, I Madé is (male) second-born, and Ni Nyoman is (female) third-born. The order of birth name also serves as the proper names for address in public.

kopi coffee.

kretek a clove cigarette.

kris dagger inscribed with signs of magical powers; typically symbolic of masculine strength.

kulit buffalo hide.

Kuningan the end of the ten-day New Year celebration, when the gods return to the heavens.

Legong a highly stylized dance performed by three prepubescent girls. There are numerous forms of Legong, most of which depict an ancient myth in an abstract way. The dancers use movement, not words, to illustrate the story.

leyak human form of evil, often manifest as an animal or ball of light.

lontar sacred texts; etched with knife on *lontar* palm leaves and inked with charcoal powder. Leaves are bound through a center hole and covered with bamboo or wood.

Mahabharata Hindu epic poem. Tells the story of the descendants of Bharata, reaching its climax in the battle between the Pandawas and Korawas. The story makes up less than a quarter of the poem, the remainder being legendary history, the science of war, ethics, fairy tales, cosmology, statecraft, philosophical interludes, and so on.

mandi bath; or, more properly, "bathing ritual."

manis sweet.

mantra a secret spoken formula of great magical power.

I must concentrate my mind
on the divine Guru Reka, Kama Tantra;
my voice is the Jewel of the eight qualities.
—Dharma Pawayangan

The power of the voice is given by the Jewel to the *dalang*, whose *mantras* serve to guide deities or ancestors downward onto the stage.

menari Indonesian word: to dance.

mimpi manis sweet dreams.

Mpu title of sage.

mudra sacred hand gesture of Hindu or Buddhist origins.

nenek an old woman.

nyingak bebek Balinese dance term: slight sideways and upward tilt of the head with simultaneous darting eye movements.

Pak Indonesian term of respect for grown man; from *bapak*, "father"; similar to "Mr."

Pandawas The five heroes of the Mahabharata: Yudistra, Bima, Arjuna, Nakala, and Sahadewa, brothers of semidivine birth. In the story they defeat their one hundred cousins, the Korawas.

parwa section; the 110,000 couplets of the Mahabharata are divided into eighteen parwas.

Parwa Hariwangsa danced dramatization adapted from the Mahabharata. The dialogue of the drama is sung in Old Javanese.

pedanda high priest; Buddhist or Hindu Brahamin caste.

pemangku secular priest.

Pendet offering dance performed by small girls.

penjor tall bamboo poles festooned with palm-leaf decorations; symbol of Dewi Sri.

pokok foundations; roots; symbolized in the oral, written, iconographic, and ceremonial tradition of Origin.

pomo May it be so.

pondok a simply made structure that serves as shelter from the weather; usually in or near the rice fields.

Prang Duri annual ritual combat with branches of the duri palm. Performed only in Tenganan village.

prau small fishing boat.

pura temple. There are three temples that are necessary to designate a coherent village: the Pura Puséh, Origins Temple; the Pura Desa, Secular or Village Temple; and the Pura Dalem, Death Temple.

puri palace; dwelling place of descendants of local prince.

raja king.

ramai busy; active; crowded (time or place); a highly desirable condition.

rebab a lute-like instrument, two-stringed.

Rejang an ancient purification dance performed only by women and young girls.

rupiah Indonesian currency; "rups" (English slang).

Sanghyang trance tradition in which the spirit of a certain god or creature manifests itself through the performer, as in Sanghyang Jaran, "horse spirit."

Sang Hyang divinity, spirit.

Sanghyang Dedari the trance dance of "heavenly nymphs."

Sang Hyang Widhi the immanent Godhead; the Totality; "That Which Is" (in Hindu terms). All gods and spirits; Wisnu, Shiwa, Brahma, Dewi Sri are manifestations of the cosmic force of the Godhead.

sarong garment worn on the lower half of the body.

sawah wet rice field.

selamat tidur blessings on your sleep.

selendang ceremonial cloth worn around the waist or chest.

Sidha Karya "One Who Makes the Ceremony Successful." Sidha Karya, whose mask is grotesque and frightening, serves as the priest of the Topéng Pajegan. His dance completes, both literally and magically, the Topéng Pajegan performance.

singha Lion. *Singha* Mega is the Great Lion.

subak a farm organization that administers irrigation.

taksu a special state of receptivity to the mysterious powers of the gods who will manifest in some form during ritual performance; the place where light, spirit, life enter; a beneficent spirit that can be controlled. Before a performance, the dancer (actor, puppeteer) will make offerings, recite *mantras*, and perform *mudras* to make contact with the *taksu* in order to be entered. "His dance was technically superb, but there was no *taksu*."

Tantri stories brought to Indonesia with the Indian tradition. In Indian version, called Panchatantra, which is related to the One-Thousand-and-One Nights cycle of fables in the Middle East. In the Balinese Tantri stories, Tantri is

	the name of the woman who tells stories to the king.	Topéng Tua	the Old Man solo pantomime; part of Topéng.
"Tat tvam asi."	Sanskrit: "I am thou and thou art I."	*tuak*	palm wine.
tenang	calm.	*tutup*	cover.
Topéng	masked dance-drama; literally, "pressed against the face." The most common theater form is performed by a company of five men, who play all the roles, interchanging characters and masks.	*warung*	food stand; may be a small table or an enclosed structure or building.
		wayang	puppet; from word meaning "shadow."
Topéng Keras	fierce masked dancer.		
Topéng Pajegan	ritual mask performance; sacred solo dance involving numerous masks all performed by one actor. Must culminate with performance of Sidha Karya.		

Hence the trees change into shadows,
and the spirit of the ancestors
animates the living world.
—MPU TAN AKUNG
twelfth-century song

wayang kulit	shadow-puppet theater.

BIBLIOGRAPHY

Artaud, Antonin — *The Theater and Its Double*, New York: Grove Press, 1958.

Bali Post — "Nyoman Kakul: Man of Many Faces," Denpasar, Bali, Sept. 24, 1978.

Ballinger, Rucina — "Status in Bali and the Penasar," Honolulu: University of Hawaii, 1977 (manuscript).

Bateson, Gregory, and Holt, Claire — "Form and Function of the Dance in Bali," *The Function of Dance in Human Society*, New York: Boas School, 1944.

Belo, Jane — *Traditional Balinese Culture*, New York: Columbia University Press, 1970.

Boas, Franziska — *The Function of Dance in Human Society*, New York: Boas School, 1944.

Covarrubias, Miguel — *Island of Bali*, New York: Alfred A. Knopf, 1937.

de Kleen, Tyra — *Mudras: The Ritual Hand Poses of the Buddha Priests and the Shiva Priests of Bali*, London: K. Paul, Trench, Trubner and Co., 1924.

de Zoete, Beryl, and Spies, Walter — *Dance and Drama in Bali*, London: Faber and Faber, 1938; reprinted London: Oxford University Press, 1973.

Deren, Maya — *Divine Horsemen*, New York: Dell Publishing Co., 1970.

Emigh, John — "Playing with the Past: Ancestral Visitation and Dramatic Illusion in the Mask Theater of Bali," *The Drama Review*, New York University School of the Arts, June 1970.

Fuller-Snyder, Allegra — "Levels of Event Patterns: An Attempt to Find the Place of Dance in a Wholistic Context," 1974. (Monograph delivered at Asian Dance Art Conference, Honolulu, 1978.)

Geertz, Clifford — *The Interpretation of Cultures*, New York: Basic Books, 1973.

Gralapp, Leland W. — *Balinese Painting*, The Taylor Museum of the Colorado Springs Fine Arts Center, 1961.

Hooykaas, C. — "Counsel and Advice to the Souls of the Dead," *Review of Indonesian and Malaysian Affairs*, Vol. 10, No. 1, January–February, 1976.

I Madé Bandem — *Baris*, Konservatori Karawitan / Indonesia Jurusan Bali di Denpasar, 1977.

I Madé Bandem and I Nyoman Rembang — *Topéng-Bali / Seni Pertunjukkan*, Proyek Penggalian, Pemtanaan Pengembangan Seni Klasik / Tradisionil dan Kesenian Baru Pemerintah Daerah, Tingkat, Bali, 1976.

McPhee, Colin — "Dance in Bali," *Dance Index*, ed. Lincoln Kirstein and Marian Eames, Vol. VII, 1949.

McPhee, Colin — *Music in Bali*, New Haven, Conn.: Yale University Press, 1966.

Mead, Margaret, and Bateson, Gregory — *Balinese Character: A Photographic Analysis*, New York, New York Academy of Sciences, 1942.

Moebirman — *Wayang Purwa: The Shadow Play of Indonesia*, Jakarta, Java: Yayasan Pelita Wisata, 1973; The Hague: Van Deventer Maasstichting, 1973.

Parabola: Myth and the Quest for Meaning, "Sacred Dance," Vol. IV, No. 2, ed. D. M. Dooling, The Society for the Study of Myth and Tradition, New York, May 1979.

Stuart-Fox, David J. — *The Art of the Balinese Offering*, Jogjakarta, Java: Penerbitan Yayasan Kanisius, 1974.

Walker, Benjamin — *The Hindu World, An Encyclopedic Survey of Hinduism*, New York: Frederick A. Praeger, 1968.

Wallis, Richard H. — "Balinese Theatre: Coping with the Old and New," *Proceedings from the Fourth Conference on Indonesia: What Is Modern Indonesian Culture?* Athens: Ohio University Press, 1980.

ACKNOWLEDGMENTS

To I Nyoman Kakul and his family for boundless inspiration, courage, and love. To Jacob Samuel for collaboration and companionship, and for being always in my heart.

To Pedanda Dawan for spiritual guidance. To Pemanku I Ketut Regig of Tegalalang for illumination of voice. To I Ketut Suparta for assistance in translation of the Tantri stories. To the Indonesian Ministry of Culture for gracious assistance in all bureaucratic matters. To the Department of Immigration, Bali, for facilitating my stay and work. To all members of ASTI, Indonesian Dance Academy, Bali, for support of photographic documentation. To Pak Tempo and his family, Tampaksiring, Bali, for contact with ancestral spirits. In New York, to the Lincoln Center Dance Committee for its endorsement of the work in its early stages.

To Leslie Holzer for unfailing encouragement. To Leonard Pitt, Rucina Ballinger, and Hadipoernomo for staunch friendship and insightful dialogue on the motivation of dance/movement. To Sardono for stimulating discussion. To Richard Wallis, Mary Zurbuchen, Mark Poffenberger, and David Stuart-Fox for scholarly guidance, a wing, and a prayer. To Tom Vinetz and Nancy Mozur for lending an ear. To Alan Wertheimer for friendship. To Bart Cannistra, Bonita Rosenbloom, and Daniel Zimbaldi for consultation and assistance in editing and layout of the photographs. To Stephen Acronico for leaps of faith and trust. To John Coy and JoWynne Markham for preparation of the initial presentation. To Judith Samuel, Barbara Miller, Andrew Richter, and Dorothy Schuler for assistance and counsel on the manuscript. To Graphic Process Color Laboratory, Los Angeles, for perfect color transparencies. To Janet Shipper, Harry Zeitlin, and Jacob Samuel for immaculate black-and-white prints.

To Andrea Oberstone, Bob Sharp, Dinah Mellon, and Bond Wright for loving-kindness and guidance. To my mother, Betty Daniel, for weaving me into the fabric of life and providing me with my winter coat. To R. Buckminster Fuller for the link across time and space. To Dr. Margaret Mead for steering me clear of treacherous waters. To Nicolas Slonimsky for instructions in tending the "Garden of the Happy Dead."

To Leslie Holzer, J.L. Thomas, Iris M. Gaynor, Loren, Liba, and Ann Madsen, Electra Yourke, Larry Hoff, José and Paul Reynard, Jean Sulzberger, Steve Schwartz, and Sara Jane Fryman for generous hospitality and accommodations in New York.

To all those at Knopf and Random House who so efficiently produced this book, especially to Bob Gottlieb for patience and wise counsel. To Ellen McNeilly for initiation into the printer's language. To Elissa Ichiyasu for steadfast execution and consideration. To Bob Scudellari for use of the light box, and to my editor, Karen Latuchie, for constant reassurance.